THE APOSTOLIC CHURCH ADVANCING

A TRIUMPHANT KINGDOM

THE APOSTOLIC CHURCH ADVANCING

ROBERT HEIDLER & CHUCK D. PIERCE

GZI
PUBLISHING

Published by Glory of Zion International Ministries, Inc.
PO Box 1601
Denton, Texas 76202
gloryofzion.org

© 2019 by Robert Heidler and Chuck D. Pierce

All rights reserved. No part of this publication may be reproduced, stored in a retrieval system, or transmitted in any form or by any means - for example, electronic, photocopy, recording - without prior written permission of the publisher. The only exception is brief quotations.

All scripture quotations, unless otherwise indicated, are taken from the *New King James Version*. Copyright 1979, 1980, 1982 by Thomas Nelson, Inc. Used by permission. All rights reserved.

Other versions used are:
AMP - Scripture taken from The Amplified Bible, Old Testament copyright © 1965, 1987 by the Zondervan Corporation. The Amplified New Testament copyright © 1958, 1987 by The Lockman Foundation. Used by permission.
NIV - Scripture taken from The Holy Bible, New International Version®. Copyright © 1973, 1978, 1984 by International Bible Society. Used by permission of Zondervan Publishing House, all rights reserved.
NASB - Scripture taken from The New American Standard Bible. Old Testament © 1971 by The Lockman Foundation. New Testament © 1963 by The Lockman Foundation. Used by permission. All rights reserved.
"Scripture quotations marked TPT are from The Passion Translation ®.
Copyright © 2017 by BroadStreet Publishing® Group, LLC.
Used by permission. All rights reserved. thePassionTranslation.com

ISBN 13: 978-1-7340661-0-4

Cover Design: Glory of Zion International

CONTENTS

FOREWORD

PART ONE: PROPHETIC INTRODUCTION *(by Chuck D. Pierce)*

CHAPTER 1: Understand and Know How to Redeem the Times! 3

CHAPTER 2: A New Watchman Movement Has Begun! 27

CHAPTER 3: Advancing in the War Ahead! 47

PART TWO: THE CHURCH JESUS PLANTED *(by Robert Heidler)*

CHAPTER 4: The Church We've Known 73

CHAPTER 5: Searching for Revival 75

CHAPTER 6: A Church in Perpetual Revival 81

CHAPTER 7: The Miraculous Church 89

PART THREE: KEYS FOR A SUPERNATURAL CHURCH *(by Robert Heidler)*

CHAPTER 8: Pastoral or Apostolic? 103

CHAPTER 9: A Picture of Five-Fold Ministry 111

CHAPTER 10: Apostolic Centers 117

PART FOUR: A STRATEGY TO ADVANCE *(by Robert Heidler)*

CHAPTER 11: The Celebration 123

CHAPTER 12: The Synaxis 133

CHAPTER 13: A Visit to a First Century Synaxis 141

PART FIVE: RAISING UP A SUPERNATURAL CHURCH *(by Robert Heidler)*

CHAPTER 14: Taking Up Your Power Tools 151

CHAPTER 15: Six Things You Need to Know about Spiritual Gifts 157

CHAPTER 16: A Growth Environment for the Gifts 173

CHAPTER 17: The Apostolic Church and the Last-Days Revival 183

APPENDIX ONE: How to Be Baptized in the Holy Spirit 189

APPENDIX TWO: The Gifts of the Spirit 207

APPENDIX THREE: Establishing a Synaxis 217

FOREWORD

by Robert Heidler

There is nothing in the world more important to Jesus than His Church. The Church is the object of Jesus' love, and the central focus of His work. In Ephesians 5:25, Paul describes Jesus' love for the church as the fervent love of a groom for his bride. He tells us: "Christ *loved* the church and gave Himself up for her."

Why is the church so important to Jesus? It's because the church is God's only plan to rescue humanity from the oppression of Satan and to bring men and women into a love relationship with Himself.

God established the church as a supernatural organism, and in its early years, the rulers of Hell had no power against it.

In the Dark Ages, however, the church compromised with paganism and lost God's power, but God did not give up on His church.

Beginning in the 15th century, God began an incredible work of restoration. It began with the Protestant Reformation, and continued through the Great Awakenings, the Pentecostal and Charismatic Movements, and many other times of Holy Spirit visitation. Through these moves of the Spirit, the church has experienced a significant measure of restoration.

The first decade of the 20th century saw the restoration of the gift of tongues. Moving through the 20th Century, we saw healing restored, prophecy restored, and the apostolic restored. In the 21st Century we've seen more and more churches begin to function in true 5-fold ministry and the return of apostolic centers. (I'll explain more about that in a future chapter.)

But while much has been restored, the restoration is not yet complete. God's goal is to *fully* restore the church. God wants to have a church that operates in New Testament power, where signs and wonders take place, believers live in God's blessing and the harvest is brought in. We are privileged to live in the days when these things *are* being restored.

This is an exciting time to be in the church. God is doing an incredible work in our day. I believe we are the generation that will experience the full restoration of the church.

Chuck and I have written a three book trilogy to help you gain a clear vision of what God is doing in our day. They are:

1. *The Messianic Church Arising!* – The restoration of the church's **COVENANT ROOTS** (The foundation for a multi-generational revival.)

2. *The Apostolic Church Arising!* – The **APOSTOLIC STRUCTURE** of the early church. (Understanding five-fold ministry and apostolic centers.)

3. *A Triumphant Kingdom: The Apostolic Church Advancing!* (This book) The **APOSTOLIC STRATEGY** of the early church – (How the early church advanced against the enemy and changed the world.)

Our prayer is that as you read this book, you will gain a fresh vision for what God is doing, and clear direction to move forward in faith to experience supernatural Christianity.

Part 1

Prophetic Introduction

by Chuck D. Pierce

1

I Will Have A People Who Understand and Know How to Redeem the Times!

There is a moment when time makes a shift and you gain momentum for your future. We are in that Kingdom moment now. We have not just entered a new season, but a new era in the Kingdom of God. In Isaiah 32:1, the Word of God says, *"Look – a new **era** begins! A king will reign in righteousness, and his princes according to justice!"* (TPT) We are now entering a new era. An era is a fixed point in time from which a series of years is reckoned. An era can also be a memorable or important date or event in the history of a thing, person, or nation. An era is a system of chronological notation computed from a given date as basis. An era is a period identified by some prominent figure or characteristic feature or stage in development. **We are now entering a new Kingdom era.**

A Time to See, Refine Vision, and Decree Your Future!

Without a vision, a people perish. In Proverbs 29:18, this word actually means that without boundaries or prophetic utterance a people go backwards. We are hoping this book will give you great vision for the future. *We are moving from a* **Church** *era to a* **Kingdom** *era.* In this divine shift, the Lord is transforming our mindset so we move outwardly from what has been built in one season, into a new movement for the next season. This will be a new building season, but first we must unlock God's Kingdom plan and align heaven and earth.

When the Lord revealed His Messiahship to His disciples in Matthew 16, He gave Peter a prophetic word that would transcend the ages. Matthew 16:18-19 says, *"And I say to you that you are Peter, and on this rock I will build My church; and the gates of Hades (death) will not overpower it [by preventing the resurrection of the Christ]. I will give you the keys (authority) of the kingdom of heaven; and whatever you bind [forbid, declare to be improper and unlawful] on earth will have [already] been bound in heaven, and whatever you loose [permit, declare lawful] on earth will have [already] been loosed in heaven."* (AMP) Though the prophet Isaiah had prophesied something very similar (Is. 22:22), we must understand that there would be an exchange of keys that would produce an authority in the Kingdom. We must also remember that this prophecy to Peter had yet to be fully revealed in reality. *The Church was still a mystery.* Therefore, when the day of Pentecost came and 3,000 were converted, Peter must have thought, *"How will we build for the future? How will the Lord, who has ascended, accomplish this through us?"*

The disciples did not have a full concept of the meaning of the "Church". The only concept they had of spiritual gathering was from the synagogue. The word the Lord was using here was *ecclesia*, which was a Roman concept of ambassadors going in to transform a region to make it look like Rome. Everything seemed new to the disciples. Just a few weeks prior, they had a revelation of the Lord being Messiah. Now they had to see how to gather and build for the future out of a new paradigm. Eventually they would have to leave Jerusalem to do this, and build in Antioch a prototype of what the Lord was prophesying. The writer of Hebrews gave us much revelation of how what the Spirit of God was doing in that day could not be done in Jerusalem.

This would begin a whole new era. Now, the *Spirit of God* would help His leadership establish something that would be indestructible. There would be unsurpassed power in the ecclesia to overcome the enemy of mankind, Satan. And before this was built, there had to be an unlocking of God's Kingdom power within the triumphant people that would walk into the future. We must remember it took approximately 70 years to establish the first Church era. In every era, we unlock a Kingdom plan so that we can build the prototype for the ecclesia for the future. This new era propels us into a season of unlocking so that we can build in days ahead.

The Glory Shift!

Once you taste and experience the Glory of God, nothing else will satisfy you. His glory is the weightiness or heaviness of His honor, splendor, power, wealth, authority, magnificence, fame, dignity, riches and excellency resting upon us, or in our atmosphere. His glory is so real that it is tangible. His glory is the opposite of the vanity of the world. Eventually, His Glory will fill the earth. As the prophet Habakkuk says in 3:3, *"His glory covered the heavens, and the earth was full of His praise."* He began his prophecy by saying, *"For I will work a work in your days which you would not believe though it were told you."* (1:5, NKJV) The Lord's original purpose in our creation was for us to live in His glory. Garden life represented both work and worship engulfed by God's glory. We are on the verge of a great glory shift. This will cause God's Kingdom triumphant people to be recognized in a new way. As Yeshua says, they will perform miracles and works even beyond the things that were seen in His day.

A shift entails a scheduled time and includes an exchange or replacement of one thing for another. A shift can be described as a change of gear allowing you to accelerate. A shift can also be an underhanded or deceitful scheme. Therefore, we must recognize that the enemy is plotting to stop the shift the Lord intends for us to make in this new era. Much shaking will occur during this shift. Change that produces shifts can also produce rifts.

Over this last season, there has been great warfare to refine our vision. The Spirit of God has been breaking captivity from the promises that have been spoken in other generations. In this last season, we have seen many angels intervene to assist us both with messages and divine intervention of circumstances. We have seen many relationships change and alignments form for the future. Now we are feeling the birth pangs for the future. The first question is, *"Do we have the strength to bring forth God's plan for harvest throughout the nations?"* Another question is, *"Will we cross fully in manifestation and demonstration of His glory, or will we postpone this manifestation for another generation?"* One final question is, *"Are we ready to be commissioned and sent into the harvest fields ahead?"*

When God's manifest presence invades our daily lives, things change! We cannot remain the same. Either we will harden our hearts as the Israelites did on many occasions or experience new *zoe* life. If we choose to allow God's presence to soften our hearts, then we may see the power of God released in greater measure. We may catch a glimpse of the very atmosphere of heaven. We experience God! He longs to pour out His glory upon His people so that we may know Him. This experience is not just for us personally but for the harvest of souls the Lord would draw in through the magnetic influence His presence has on the lost.

There is Such a War Over the Manifest Presence of God

There has always been a war over the glory or the ark becoming central in our lives and ministries. There will always be a war in this arena. We will talk more about this in the next chapter. One of my favorite verses is 2 Corinthians 3:18: *"But we all, with unveiled face, beholding as in a mirror the glory of the Lord, are being transformed into the same image from glory to glory, just as by the Spirit of the Lord."*

The question comes up: why is it necessary to move from glory to glory? Isn't one glory as good as the next? *The answer is no,* because in every season of glory we experience a new order that God brings to our lives as we mirror His image to a greater extent. But then we begin to add a new method—a settled plan or strategy of how we operate within that new order. It is our way of implementing what we have learned from God.

While in and of itself this is not a problem, we can eventually get so organized in God's last manifestation of glory that the enemy can use it to hold us back from God's next step for us. It is very easy to become legalistic or build binding doctrines around a truth that God revealed during a past season of glory. That, however, can leave us open to not moving forward when it comes time for God to change the seasons in our lives. If we do not allow God to move us from glory to glory, we will get caught up living in an old season.

As the Holy Spirit moves us toward becoming more Christ-like, the methodology of an old season will not propel us into the future. We need something new and fresh. We need a new glory. This is one of the wiles of the enemy - to hold us captive in the last manifestation of God. Therefore, we are captive to the past rather than moving into the best that is ahead for our lives. This is how religious spirits operate.

There is a Plan of Triumphant Redemption for Each Believer

Did you know that you have a portion specifically allotted to you from God? The word *inheritance* means "my portion." We have all been given a space, territory, or arena in which we have been granted authority. That is our portion, and how we steward it is key to our success in the spirit realm. In fact, the climate of our domain reflects our relationship with the Lord; therefore, our chief desire should be for the presence of the Holy God to occupy our inheritance. You must learn to war to see His presence in your sphere of authority.

There is a great war over the inheritance of our future. Many times, our warfare is centered around internal issues. Like Peter, we are having to get beyond ourselves so that we can be sent into God's mission and the destiny that He has for us. Another thing to understand is gaining access to enter your ***breakthrough portal!*** Gain access to the council necessary to war for the promise ahead! Enter with a MIND to TRIUMPH! If you are moving in the new, you will see several changes: His fullness will be seen in your personality; your soul will be restored from the last season; all fear and manipulation that have crowded your identity and confined you to your past will leave your personality; your new identity will reflect His ability to overcome the mountains that stopped your progress (see Isaiah 41 and Zechariah 4). He has given you power over the enemies that would hinder your progress (see 2 Corinthians 10:3–6). Gain ACCESS and steer the course of history with your prayers and acts of faith.

Through the Son's death, He paid for your access. He is now seated at the right hand of Father, ready to give you access to triumphant counsel. Before we were ever conceived or knit together in our mothers' wombs, God had a distinct plan for our life. He destined us before the foundation of the earth. He knew the timing in which we would be born, and the generation of which we would be a part. He had a purpose for us and knew what would be necessary to accomplish that purpose in the earth, within that time frame. We are all born in that chosen time and season. Upon our conception, God's redemptive plan began for our life. Our life cycle, designed by God, began at the point of conception and continues through birth, age of accountability, our spiritual rebirth, maturing faith, and death, before entering eternity. The process requires wisdom and counsel for each one of us to walk victoriously. In Proverbs 4:18 we find, *"The way or path of righteousness is like the first gleam of dawn or as a shining light, which shines ever brighter until the full light of day."*

When thinking about our redemptive path, our Redeemer has already paid the price for us to walk victoriously through life. To redeem means to pay the required price, or to secure the release of a convicted criminal. Our Redeemer is the person making that payment. Therefore, Jesus has already redeemed us from the darkness in our path of life. Psalm 16:11 says, *"You will show me the path of life; in your presence is fullness of joy; at your right hand are pleasures forevermore."* We must know that we have access to His wisdom, power and glory.

A New Dimension of Glory in a New Apostolic Season!

Behold, I do a new thing! Isaiah 43:18-21 says, *"Stop dwelling on the past. Don't even remember these former things. I am doing something brand new, something unheard of. Even now it sprouts and grows and matures. Don't you perceive it? I will make a way in the wilderness and open up flowing streams in the desert. Wild beasts, jackals, and owls will glorify me. For I supply streams of water in the desert and rivers in the wilderness to satisfy the thirst of my people, my chosen ones, so that you, whom I have shaped and formed for myself, will proclaim my praise."* (TPT)

In my book *A Time to Triumph*, I fully explain the concept of a "new mindskin for a new wineskin".[1] After the Lord prophesied to Peter, Peter had a hard time shifting his thought process to understand that the Messiah still had to complete His mission on earth to redeem mankind. He actually attempted to stop the Lord from going back to Jerusalem. The Lord had prophesied His crucifixion, death, and resurrection. Neither Peter's mind nor emotions could fathom the Lord allowing this to happen, even though he just had a revelation of who He was. The Lord actually equated Peter's identity to that of Satan when He said, "Get behind me, Satan." He knew Satan would do anything to stop the redemption of mankind. When we stop progressing into the new, our thinking gets confused and skewed. Peter had to go through much shifting and sifting to come into the future.

When the Lord submitted Himself to the cross through death, He first descended into hell to unlock the prisoners. Ephesians 4:7-16 is very key to understand the era that we are living in.

> *Yet grace [God's undeserved favor] was given to each one of us [not indiscriminately, but in different ways] in proportion to the measure of Christ's [rich and abundant] gift. Therefore, it says, "When He ascended on high, He led captivity captive, and He bestowed gifts on men." (Now this ex-*

pression, "He ascended," what does it mean except that He also had previously descended [from the heights of heaven] into the lower parts of the earth? He who descended is the very same as He who also has ascended high above all the heavens, that He [His presence] might fill all things [that is, the whole universe]). And [His gifts to the church were varied and] He Himself appointed some as apostles [special messengers, representatives], some as prophets [who speak a new message from God to the people], some as evangelists [who spread the good news of salvation], and some as pastors and teachers [to shepherd and guide and instruct], [and He did this] to fully equip and perfect the saints (God's people) for works of service, to build up the body of Christ [the church]; until we all reach oneness in the faith and in the knowledge of the Son of God, [growing spiritually] to become a mature believer, reaching to the measure of the fullness of Christ [manifesting His spiritual completeness and exercising our spiritual gifts in unity]. So that we are no longer children [spiritually immature], tossed back and forth [like ships on a stormy sea] and carried about by every wind of [shifting] doctrine, by the cunning and trickery of [unscrupulous] men, by the deceitful scheming of people ready to do anything [for personal profit]. But speaking the truth in love [in all things—both our speech and our lives expressing His truth], let us grow up in all things into Him [following His example] who is the Head—Christ. From Him the whole body [the church, in all its various parts], joined and knitted firmly together by what every joint supplies, when each part is working properly, causes the body to grow and mature, building itself up in [unselfish] love." (AMP)

He first descended, so that He could ascend. Upon His ascension He gave the necessary gifts for mankind that would enforce the victory He had just won. Mankind was to align and operate in those gifts from age to age so His victorious Church would fully unlock His Kingdom in the earth. This Kingdom would reflect heaven's rule in the earth realm (the Lord's Prayer).

The Difference Between Kingdom and Church

We need to understand the difference between Kingdom and Church. The Kingdom is the whole of God's redeeming activity in Christ in the world. He oversees and reviews what Kingdom strategies of His are manifesting in the seven-mountain structure of society. The Church is the assembly of those who belong to Christ Jesus. Dutch Sheets puts it this way: "Kingdom takes visible form in those who have assembled as the Church." As we make this shift in our understanding, we will start manifesting the Kingdom. When we assemble, we should have a much greater power than that which we exhibit alone. We need to ask God to shift us into a greater holy array so that He can come and meet us in a new way.

Kingdom people are sent out to do Kingdom work. As Kingdom representatives advance, they will meet opposing forces. Kingdom people know warfare and do not back off from it. They know that kingdoms are in conflict and have learned to maneuver in the warfare of the Kingdom. They are not trying to protect themselves. They are on a mission every time they leave their front doors. We have been given grace and faith to overcome the anti-Christ forces.

The Spirit of God is now developing centers where a Kingdom display can occur. The Lord not only declares His Word, but He performs His Word and manifests His glory. These apostolic centers are prototypes of heaven for all the earth to see.

In *The Apostolic Church Arising,*[2] a recent book by Robert Heidler and me, we explain the characteristics of the Kingdom, which many do not understand. Often people relate the concept of kingdom to worldly structures, but that is not the highest level of Kingdom rule. When you begin with the way God set up His Kingdom, the world will not be able to conform you to a lower expression of kingdom. Here are the characteristics of a Kingdom-minded entity advancing in the earth:

- ◆ *Kingdom has a government.* We see the importance of government in the Kingdom in the Jesus Movement of the 1960s. God brought multitudes into His Kingdom, but there was no government in place to secure the harvest. Though many came in, much of that harvest was lost. Kingdom must have a supernatural government: we must understand Lord Sabaoth, the Lord of Hosts. We must understand how Jehovah-Nissi sends His government into war.
- ◆ *Kingdom is ruled by a king.* We must not forget that our King has sovereign rule over His government. He can promote you or set you on a shelf for a year. We submit to earthly rulers, but when we understand all authority structures, we can maneuver in them as representatives of the Kingdom of God.
- ◆ *Kingdom has administration.* Kingdom administration is different than church administration to which we have been accustomed. Administration can be difficult to grasp, but it is vital. To come into all that God wants, we must understand the Church's role in the Kingdom. You cannot express Kingdom by doing as Israel did at the end of the book of Judges, when all the people "did what was

right in their own eyes." People who refuse to discover their places or positions in a new season cannot operate in the ultimate Kingdom expression God desires for them.

- *Kingdom has a culture.* If we conform to the cultures around us and never learn Kingdom culture, we will fail. We have lived at a lower level than what God wants for us because we have not expressed the culture of the Kingdom. Kingdom culture is higher than those of the world.

- *Kingdom is good news.* Kingdom is an alignment with the One who is giving us access from the throne. He who died for us and overcame all powers and principalities is now mediating for us to display His authority in the earth. This is good news for the world. If we do not demonstrate God's rule in the earth realm, we are not being the ambassadors God is calling us to be. Because Kingdom requires a corporate response, our gifts must align and be ordered before certain demonic forces can be overcome.

- *Kingdom is connected through generations.* In our culture, young people are usually focused on establishing their own lives; the danger is that they can miss Kingdom authority. One of the cries of my heart is for the next generation to grasp the meaning of Kingdom. The Kingdom of God is within us, but we must understand that we must connect to the generation before and after us. God is a tri-generational God. Therefore, for a new generation to arise successfully, they must understand their history.

- *God's heavenly Kingdom is not based on worldly patterns.* This causes some people to be confused about salvation. I think more people are saved than we realize, but not all of them enter into Kingdom. A heart for God does not equal expressing Kingdom in the earth. If you do not understand Kingdom, you become judgmental and critical as you see people striving to work out their salvation.

- *God's Kingdom is beyond man's natural thoughts.* The Bible says that the Kingdom cannot be comprehended by the natural mind. You have to get Kingdom from a supernatural dimension; it must be revealed. Ask the Lord to bring you into a higher level of Kingdom understanding.
- *Kingdom cannot be obtained by ambition.* Remember when the "Sons of Thunder" tried to do just that? Even their mother was ambitious. This is not a good thing. Nor it is when a wife or husband tries to force a spouse into a more spiritual place. Ambition is a mean demon. This is what Judas had; he was ambitious for the Kingdom, but his ambition shifted him out of the eternal structure that he had been offered and into a role that led to destruction.
- *Kingdom should never be postponed.* When God is ready, He will move. The culture shock of moving between kingdoms can get you in a mess, however. We have to ask the Lord to keep us abreast of the way He is moving and learn how to represent Kingdom properly.
- *Kingdom has provision.* Kingdom supply structures will be one of the greatest changes we see in this shift, and we must understand them. We have garments and mantles that dress us, for we put on Christ daily.
- *Kingdom has a territory.* To establish the Kingdom in any territory, you must first develop the presence of God. This is why David's

kingdom, which operated around the Ark of the Covenant, came closest to reflecting the pattern of heaven. God's presence was established in the Tabernacle of David because God was enthroned on the praises of Israel. If you put Church above Kingdom, you will develop the "gathering" structure as your priority rather than the "presence" structure. You will not be driven by God's presence; instead you will end up being program-driven to meet the needs of the people. Eventually, the people will still have to move into the presence of God to succeed.

- *Kingdom has an atmosphere.* Unless God's presence is established, you will not move forward. Beginning with God's presence is more difficult, because it cannot be understood from the world's perspective. The world understands "gathering" to meet people's needs. A church can look not much different from the world—gathering for fellowship, enjoying each other and meeting people. But if you are presence-driven, meeting needs is not a driving motivation. This is the key to the seven mountains of human society; we move from God's Kingdom into the structures of the world.

- *Kingdom has prophets.* God ordains people who represent Him in every aspect of His authority. David had recorders and scribes, and so do I. At our ministry, Glory of Zion, the recorders and scribes record everything we do, as well as significant dreams, because I value God's word and its expression.

- *Kingdom has war units.* God's Kingdom people war against demonic forces. This is the difference between Kingdom and our traditional concept of church. You can "go to church" without ever going to war, and you can have great fellowship with people but never war with them. At Glory of Zion, we have war units who will gather for intercession at 3:00 A.M., if God calls us to war during that watch. This is a military unit meeting with God, to gain strategy to overcome the enemy.

- ◆ *Kingdom has gatekeepers.* Some gatekeepers can be challenging. I have had gatekeepers check my name tag before letting me into a conference! But this is the function of gatekeepers: They question who is coming in and out of the gate. Gatekeepers fulfill what Jesus prophesied in Matthew 16 about the gates of hell. They have the ability to bind, to forbid, or to permit. This is where we have authority when the Lord is executing His Kingdom plans in the earth.

- ◆ *Kingdom has treasurers.* The greatest warfare is in the treasury; therefore, we establish those who can serve as treasurers. They have to understand and be accountable for key information and resources.

- ◆ *Kingdom has music and sound.* I love "free for all" dance, but at times the dance has to represent an order. If you have expressive corporate dance, it must be interpreted just like tongues. If sound and dance are not interpreted, then there is something lacking in Kingdom demonstration.

- ◆ *Kingdom has people who serve as the priests and Levites did.* The sanctuary would not have been cared for, were it not for the Levites. At Glory of Zion, we have one of the most incredible Levitical structures in the world. If it did not function so efficiently, we could not do what we do. Recently, one of our retired widows dusted everything in the sanctuary. God notices this and makes sure the Levites are cared for properly. In Kingdom rule, you do not have to worry about being taken care of.

- *Kingdom has chief ministers.* I am extremely thankful for the chief ministers God has established at Glory of Zion who minister and help others minister. They have gone through much and have testimonies of overcoming.
- *Kingdom has power.* A new power and anointing are being infused from Heaven into those representing the Kingdom in earth. This power produces demonstration and causes a manifestation of glory.

We are Entering into a Divine Return to Kingdom Advancement

When you look at the foundation of the Church, you find that Jesus is the Cornerstone. Added to that cornerstone is a divine ordered gift-mix that must be aligned properly for us to triumph. The first gift that God gave to mankind was the gift of the apostle. That gift has the capacity to war, govern, finish, align generations, build, and send forth one generation into another season. The apostolic gift must connect to the cornerstone. This becomes the keystone alignment to build the prototype that the Lord has, from season to season and era to era, and over the last 20 years is something the Lord has been perfecting for a time such as this. Once that gift is connected properly, the other gifts, with their redeemed functions, build upon the cornerstone and the apostolic gift. Below is a graph that will help you.

Understand and Know How to Redeem the Times!

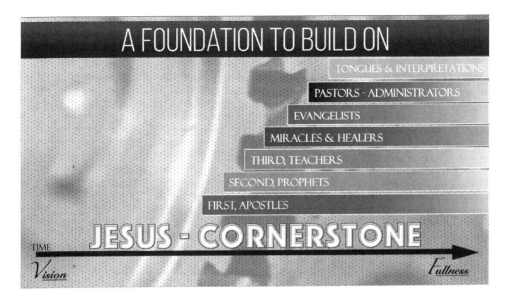

As you review this graph and God's building plan for the Church, you see that this is not a top down pyramid structure. Actually, this is the foundation for God's aligned plan for His gifts that would unlock the harvest in days ahead. Each gift must be Holy Spirit empowered. We must rely on the Holy Spirit as we enter a new season. He must become our rear guard as we advance. Unless the Holy Spirit is enfolded in the history of any land and continues directing its covenant with God, evil will overtake the society, causing the covenant root with our Creator to wither. The Holy Spirit enables us to triumph as we go through great change. In approaching the future, the real issue always concerns the change of heart and unified expression of His people, since this will release an anointing throughout the earth. The anointing breaks the yoke (see Isaiah 10:27)! God always has a triumphant reserve from generation to generation that will come forth with new strength and power.

A New Prophetic Mantle for Prophetic Revelation: From Sons of Thunder to Issachar Prophets!

The second building foundational gift is prophets. Prophets are important today. If prophets add nothing to the Word of God and change nothing that has been written, then why are they needed? Prophetically, what is recorded in the Word of God is all that is really necessary for the future generations of all ages to come. However, prophets in each generation must interpret how the revelation that has been given makes what "hath been written" coherent, cohesive, authentic and appropriate for us today.

Not only do prophets gain wisdom over how to maneuver through the world we live in, but also, they gain revelation that helps us to understand the future. God does nothing without first telling the prophets. Today, prophets have visions so they can teach, lead, exhort, chastise, warn, and encourage God's people to make right decisions. They motivate God's people to understand what He is doing today. Prophets also help us interpret and understand the times in which we are living.

The prophetic gift in the Body of Christ is now shifting from "Sons of Thunder" to "Issachar Prophets." When the Lord brought forth His covenant nation of Israel, He brought them forth by tribes or armies (Exodus 6:24). Each tribe had a particular redemptive purpose. One of the tribes, Issachar, was the tribe that understood times and seasons. The Body of Christ must be capable of *"telling time"* in the Spirit. Because of this, Robert Heidler and I began **The Issachar School**, one of the most unique schools in the Christian world.

The school has a **"One New Man Mindset"**, Jew and Gentile becoming one, with teaching from a **Hebraic** perspective. This school also teaches Kingdom of God Biblical principles which explain the government of heaven and the government of earth. The Hebraic concept of *time* is different from the way we think in the Western World. A Hebrew mindset equates the passage of time as the life cycle. The Hebrews saw man as participating in two time dimensions. First, the **"age"** of time was temporal. We have been placed in nature and we interact with the laws of science around us. The other dimension of time is "an age to come." I Corinthians 2:6-8 says, *"However, we speak wisdom among those who are mature, yet not the wisdom of this age, nor of the rulers of this age, who are coming to nothing. But we speak the wisdom of God in a mystery, the hidden wisdom which God ordained before the ages for our glory, which none of the rulers of this age knew; for had they known, they would not have crucified the Lord of glory"* (NKJV).

God has stored up wisdom for such a time as this. We can gain wisdom to which no enemy of hell has access. From a Hebraic mindset, events that occurred through life created smaller cycles of review in a bigger picture of life. When one summed up all of these smaller, temporal cycles, the finite age was determined. We are living in a time of *"summing up."* We are not just living from year to year, but when you look at the season as a whole you see the Lord doing something in our generation. He is preparing us to move more quickly and advance in His Kingdom purpose in days ahead.

I have tried to present the tribe of Issachar well in the earth today. I have a heart for God's children to know the times we are living in and what we should do to ready ourselves to advance in the earth. Issachar fully understood the long war between the House of Saul and House of David. Issachar knew how to intercede, or *"bear the burden,"* so the people could be influenced to shift properly. Issachar knew how to *open up wages necessary for Kingdom advancement* in the future. Issachar was positioned between Judah, the war and praise tribe, and Zebulun, the wealth tribe. Without understanding alignment, you do not have the right order to gain victory.

A Triumphant Move is Developing

There is a new move of God in His people this hour! They are like a river of glory fire. They resemble fiery lava moving from state to state, province to province, and nation to nation throughout the earth. These glory warriors will destroy the works of the enemy in days ahead. Over the next seven years, we will mature and be ready to go to war against the darkness attempting to bring destruction. These triumphant people are ones who know how to triumph. To *triumph* is to obtain victory, or a state of being victorious in conquest. Triumph carries a distinct emotion for God's children; in triumph, one expresses joy or exultation because he or she has prospered, succeeded and flourished.

An easy way to understand triumph is to think of a card played that takes all others ("trumping," or winning a hand or suit). Triumphant people have the following characteristics:

- **They are infused with a victorious attitude.** Attitudes, which signal the underlying emotions we have toward the tasks the Lord has given us, have a tremendous impact on how we see the world. Wrong attitudes can skew our perceptions and cloud our understanding of the fruits our labors are producing. Positioning your heart and mind on the Lord, however, will preserve you in times of trouble and lead to a victorious attitude. The Lord's triumphant people have strong hearts! Ask the Lord to adjust your attitude to triumph.
- **They are aligned for victory.** Attitude is linked with pos-

ture. Posture is linked with alignment. Posture and attitude, therefore, are linked with your positioning. An army must be aligned and ordered for victory. Alignment can be thought of as "snapping into place," the way a doctor must position a broken bone in its proper place in order for it to heal properly and the appendage to work again. God has an order, and it will not manifest until we are properly aligned. Triumphant people are snapped into alignment for victory. To create the prototype of triumph for the future, we must be aligned in God's order: first apostles, second prophets, third teachers, then healers, miracle workers, administrators, etc. Review your present alignments.

◆ **They occupy a high-level aptitude to adjust quickly.** Adapting to the needs of battle and adjusting to overcome the strategies of the enemy require aptitude. A quick ability to apprehend something is not actually dependent on your intelligence but on your attitude. Those of lesser intelligence can have the highest aptitude, and those who should have high aptitude can be sabotaged by their shoddy attitudes or lack of commitment to being aligned. We must have an attitude that enables us to adjust quickly against our enemy and toward God's order. That attitude and resulting alignment allows you to see as God sees, both the parts and how they fit together as a whole. Then, like a machine, all components are fit together exactly, allowing it to function.

◆ **They are creative, cunning (more shrewd than the enemy),**

and confrontational. Creativity and cunning are like weapons the Lord has given us to elude and overpower our enemy. But to use them effectively, we must be willing to *confront* the enemy, whether we want to or not. Consider how Jesus, led by the Spirit, confronted Satan in the wilderness: It was the bringing together of two opposing forces in which truth could be revealed through God's Word and prevail.

Triumphant Kingdom people have to be confrontive

There is not a choice. This doesn't mean they are not peacemakers. What this actually means is that there are obstacles that will hinder the advancement of God's Kingdom into harvest fields that must be confronted, for His plan to advance. In such confrontations, our creativity and cunning will give us the advantage. We will create the new from nothing. We will transform things into more prosperous forms or combine old forms into something with new qualities. And, though many Christians do not understand that they are shrewder than the powers of darkness, we will outwit the enemy by our cunning, because our covenant relationship with God allows us to. We will make strategic moves at the right time to stay ahead of the enemy, as David did when King Saul pursued him (see 1 Samuel 18:11).

In the next chapter we will look at a key vision that is manifesting today and our need to war for that vision to be fully accomplished.

Endnotes

1   Chuck D. Pierce, *A Time to Triumph*, (Chosen Books, 2016), chapter 3.

2   Chuck D. Pierce and Robert Heidler, *The Apostolic Church Arising*, (Glory of Zion International Ministries, 2015).

2

A Triumphant People Arising: A New Watchman Movement Has Begun!

God has a people who must keep moving. Movement is linked with life! If we stop moving, we stagnate or routinize. If there is one thing that I have seen happen from season to season, is that the Church stagnates. This can be because we fall into apathy. However, most times we stagnate because we enjoy getting comfortable in one season and resist change.

In a new era, we have a new identity. There are many patterns in the Word of God that reveal this. We have started discussing how the apostles had to develop a new identity of what would be known as *"the Church."* Even though the Church had been referred to throughout the Word of God, from Pentecost on, the Church became a reality. The apostles had to revert back to an understanding of corporate movement, based upon Torah. The first place you see a corporate rearrangement and movement occur is when the Lord brought the tribes out of Egypt. Exodus 6:24 says, *"... and he brought them out by armies."* This was the first time they had been gathered as tribes and would have to learn how to war together. In every new era, we must move past fear. Once Israel was moving toward their promise, they resisted their new identity. They couldn't get past the fear of the future. Therefore, they slandered their promise and even cried out to go back to their old identity.

The key to developing your new identity for the new era is to know who the Lord says you are. When you are developing a new prototype, you are really not sure who you are fully going to be. As I have discussed in other books, transition consists of moving from one place to another place. Transition has three phases: death, confusion, and advancement. You don't fully advance until you make it through the death of the past and the confusion of crossing into the new. Your mind is developing new thoughts but still has old paradigm thinking within its thought processes. Therefore, you have much internal warfare over "becoming." The enemy accuses you of your past failures to try and stop you from coming into your future triumphs.

Don't Let Your Past Stop You from Moving into the Future!

There was a whole generation of Israelites that never had the opportunity to see their promise manifest. These were leaders who actually went across and saw the reality of the promise but made a decision that the warfare to establish themselves in the promise was too great a cost. I have found that you must meditate daily on your portion of the promise that God is asking you to steward. This is what the Lord told Joshua 40 years later. I always suggest that when people are moving forward, they read Joshua 1. This chapter helps you to develop a mindset that will allow you to walk in Kingdom strategies, causing you to prosper. To triumph, we have to back away from moving beyond how the Spirit and glory of God are directing us. We must allow the "ark" to go first and give the apostolic leadership that are fully responsible to develop the prototype room to experiment.

God has deposited revelation and vision within you that will be called up for such a time as this. I believe many of those who have been a mess in the past will be the *Triumphant Reserve* for the future. Most of the Triumphant Reserve that will arise in days ahead will be those who have risen and fallen and risen again and fallen again, and only now have been labeled **"Triumphant"** as they have risen yet again. Each one made choices to follow God, no matter what the cost. Now the Lord can use them to stand steadfast and represent His Kingdom plan in the earth. *Many are coming off the shelf and being used as we advance with strength into the next harvest season! Many are "second timers" who know the power of amazing grace.*

Israel Learned to Be Triumphant

As I have said earlier, the tribes of Israel were treated as armies (Ex. 6:24). We must remember that their identity had been submerged for 400 years in the Egyptian culture. When Jacob and his son found themselves reconnecting with Joseph in Egypt, Joseph cautioned to them to not reveal their full identity. In Genesis 46, Joseph said to them, *"So it shall be, when Pharaoh calls you and says, 'What is your occupation?' that you shall say, 'Your servants' occupation has been with livestock from our youth even till now, both we and also our fathers,' that you may dwell in the land of Goshen; for every shepherd is an abomination to the Egyptians."* (NKJV)

This was a form of preserving their ethnic and spiritual identity of this people until it was God's perfect time. There comes a time for your submerged identity to rise up. Even though they had been living as slaves for 400 years, now was the time to display who they really were.

Each tribe had a distinct order and assignment. Today, many of us are unsettled because we are not positioned correctly. However, once we are properly aligned, we can find ourselves arrayed for victory. Like the Maccabees of old, the Spirit of the Lord is raising up a group (tribes) whose oil and anointing will last. This group knows how to wait and withstand the enemy. He will anoint this group with fresh oil as they use the resources they are given. They will become a perpetual, advancing, overcoming troop.

Many of this reserve had once been out of His perfect timing but now have been developed for a time such as this. These have overcome their stumbling blocks and chosen to advance beyond petty offenses. Each has come through narrow places of transition. They are a righteous troop who stand and release different types of prayers into the earth. They have reformation in their heart. They know how to be angry and sin not! Their conscience is cleansed, and they have become bold. They can go up and enter boldly into the Throne Room of Grace, gain new vision, and pave the way for many to follow. Their blood has been exchanged for His. They do not fear death. They are energized by His Spirit. This group will leap from high place to high place and always remain in their abiding place. May the Triumphant Reserve align and arise in this hour! God is calling us forth and getting us in a Holy Array! He is preparing His troops for a tremendous victory!

To triumph means to celebrate and rejoice with victory and jubilation. Triumph indicates that an advantage has been gained over the enemy. Triumph also conveys success has been granted through a supernatural grace being released. Think of the time when David triumphantly brought in the ark. The jubilation was incredible. *David danced!* He lost himself in worship because the Lord had returned the Ark of His Presence to the place of victory.

In ancient times, when an official entered the city, he was crowned with a laurel of gold, usually riding on a chariot drawn by two white horses. He could be followed by the captives from his victories. These might be defeated kings, princes, or generals with the chains of triumph around them. Psalm 149 says, *"PRAISE THE Lord! Sing to the Lord a new song, praise Him in the assembly of His saints! Let Israel rejoice in Him, their Maker; let Zion's children triumph and be joyful in their King! [Zech. 9:9; Mt. 21:5.] Let them praise His name in chorus and choir and with the [single or group] dance; let them sing praises to Him with the tambourine and lyre! For the Lord takes pleasure in His people; He will beautify the humble with salvation and adorn the wretched with victory. Let the saints be joyful in the glory and beauty [which God confers upon them]; let them sing for joy upon their beds. Let the high praises of God be in their throats and a two-edged sword in their hands, [Heb. 4:12; Rev. 1:16.] to wreak vengeance upon the nations and chastisement upon the peoples, to bind their kings with chains, and their nobles with fetters of iron, to execute upon them the judgment written. He [the Lord] is the honor of all His saints. Praise the Lord! (Hallelujah!)"* (AMP)

You can see why this passage was so important. The power of worship and sound being released sets new order in the earth. I am a worshipper. How we release sound in the earth binds the enemies with whom we are in conflict. A book series that I would suggest you read is my Future War series. This three-book series consists of *The Future War of the Church, God's Unfolding Battle Plan,* and *A Time to Triumph*[1]. One of the things we will also discuss in the next chapter is God's plan to rearrange worship in the earth realm for the new era ahead.

I decree that you will learn to triumph as you move forward into this next era.

A New Watchman Movement Has Begun: Wear a New Shamar Watchman Anointing!

If the Lord returned today, there are two things He would look for. The first is faith. Faith is linked with time and the place that God has for us. Acts 17:24-27 says, *"God, who made the world and everything in it, since He is Lord of heaven and earth, does not dwell in temples made with hands. Nor is He worshiped with men's hands, as though He needed anything, since He gives to all life, breath, and all things. And He has made from one blood every nation of men to dwell on all the face of the earth, and has determined their preappointed times and the boundaries of their dwellings, so that they should seek the Lord, in the hope that they might grope for Him and find Him, though He is not far from each one of us ..."* (NKJV) Time produces champions! The Lord shifts the times and seasons of His kingdom purposes through His people in the earth realm.

The other thing the Lord is looking for is this: are you watching after His purposes in the earth? One type of prophet is the shamar prophet. This prophet is a watchman. I have written much about this type of prophet in *The Spiritual Warfare Handbook*[2]. This type of prophet not only speaks forth but watches after the words that have been deposited in the heavens. Elijah, Jeremiah, and Daniel were all key watchman prophets. Elijah knew when it needed to rain since he prophesied it wouldn't rain for 3 ½ years. He also knew that when it was time to rain, he must intercede to pull the rain out of the heavens. Daniel found the word that Jeremiah had spoken 70 years prior and knew it was time for that word to manifest. He went into deep intercession. Angelic visitation had to occur to help him through and birth the future of the people returning to the land from which they had been taken captive. These are examples of watchman prophets. Let me share with you how the Lord caught me up, gave me a vision and how I am presently watching after that vision.

From Prayer Leader to Watchman Prophet

I was predominantly known as a Global Prayer Leader in the 1980's, 1990's, and until 2007. I was so honored that the Lord would allow me to mobilize prayer warriors all over the world. I was blessed to have had a role in directing and participating in many prayer missions. For the history of the prayer movement, you can come to the Global Prayer Tower here at the Global Spheres Center in Corinth, Texas. We have artifacts from many nations around the world and each state is represented. Dutch Sheets and I actually visited each state in America before the elections in 2004. From this tour we developed a history book (*Releasing the Prophetic Destiny of a Nation*[3]) that you can read to find God's prophetic word over every state in this nation.

One key prayer mission was in the 1990's when we sent teams to the 10/40 Window, an imaginary window that represents the area of the world most unreached by the gospel. This "window" of 69 nations spans from 10 to 40 degrees north latitude across northern Africa, the Middle East and Central Asia. This part of the world included 90% of the poorest of the poor and unreached by the Good News of the Lord Jesus Christ. Peter and Doris Wagner led the United Prayer Track, where many ministries were mobilized to pray for these people to come to know the Lord. This prayer thrust culminated in a meeting in Seoul, Korea with over 200 nations represented. This was probably the most diverse gathering in the history of the Church. I remember praying for leaders from Iran to Bangladesh and beyond. Since that time, the Church has been birthed in most of these nations. We continue to send teams to follow up and minister. I was recently in northern India. In the 1990's, you could count the leaders of that region on your fingers. In 2014, the team I took northern to India ministered to over 1500 leaders and many converts.

After the 10/40 Window thrust, we focused on sending teams to the 40/70 Window. This is an area of the earth that spans from Iceland in the west to Great Britain, through northern and Eastern Europe and includes all of Russia. Some of the greatest financial wealth in the world is controlled from within this window. Our focus was to stir up prayer in nations that experienced the Spirit of God in other generations and had a church history, but over the years, a cold hardness had entered God's people and their fire had waned. We sent teams to all 72 nations associated with this region of the world.

However, in September 2007, when attending a meeting of prophets and apostles from around the world, I was asked to share what I would be doing in the future. When my time came to share, the Spirit of God instructed me that my season as a Prayer Leader had ended, and I was to lay down that identity and await Him to bring me my next assignment. Was I to quit praying? Of course not! But my identity had to change. I had to receive His directive from heaven so that I could pray more effectively. Change can be difficult, but when we obey, we see the Lord in a new way. One thing I have learned is this: when we wait on the Lord, He will renew our strength and give us our call for the future.

From Prayer to Mobilizing an Army!

I travel extensively, explaining the shift that is taking place in the earth realm. We are moving from just being a prayer army into an army of mighty, watching warriors. Through the years, I have visited over 130 nations. Dutch Sheets and I went to all 50 states of America after the beginning of this new millennium. I have since gone back to nearly every state, some multiple times, since then. A couple of years ago we did gatherings in 22 key cities in America. Our most recent venture of mobilizing a great warring army has been to go to 22 regions in America. I will use the following as an example but know this: The Lord will have a house of prayer and an incredible remnant in every people group. Isaiah 56:7-8 says, "'*These I will bring to my holy mountain and give them joy in my house of prayer. Their burnt offerings and sacrifices will be accepted on my altar; for my house will be called a house of prayer for all nations.' The Sovereign Lord declares— he who gathers the exiles of Israel: 'I will gather still others to them besides those already gathered.'*" (NKJV)

Our goal is to raise up this triumphant remnant throughout the world. The Lord gave me a vision of the Triumphant Reserve in 2008. I want to repeat that vision here so that you see the progress that has been made since then. The word *remnant* is the same word linked with a seed. His seed will always triumph. There will always be someone He is using to advance His throne from heaven into the earth realm. I am now seeing this triumphant reserve arise in our nation and other nations throughout the earth.

God Has a Triumphant Reserve!

From September 2007 through the fall, winter and even into the spring of 2008, I just continued to minister as the Lord led me. I love ministering to God's people. We are a peculiar, precious people in the earth. However, on May 31, 2008, something happened that has changed my life to this day. I had been asked by John and Sheryl Price, Peter and Trisha Roselle, and the state leadership of New Jersey to come to Liberty Park and "open the gates in 2008" for the glory of God to flood across America. Historically, many of those who settled the East Coast, and much of the United States, arrived on Ellis Island, recorded their arrival to be part of this nation, and then caught a train that would take them to Newark or New York City.

The leadership team rented the train station at Liberty State Park, and we were to use it for a worship gathering. Before the regional meeting started, I could feel the Spirit of God moving on me. When worship began, the Spirit of God fell on me and I was caught up into a heavenly place. I began to receive a vision from the Lord for the future.

I Saw A Triumphant People Arising!

The Lord raised me and showed me the nation of the United States of America. First, He revealed His remnant and where they were positioned. Next, He showed me their strength from state to state to state in America. I said, "Lord, what are you showing me?" Like iron to a magnet, this troop began to come from every place in their state, gathering together to form what looked like a glory fire river. I said, Lord, "Who are these people?" He said, ***"This is My Triumphant Reserve for the future!"***

AS I explained earlier, to **TRIUMPH** is to obtain victory or a state of being victorious in conquest. Triumph carries a distinct emotion for God's children. In triumph, one expresses joy or exaltation because they have prospered, succeeded, and flourished! An easy way to understand triumph is a card played that takes all others (like "trumping" and winning a hand or suit). A **RESERVE** is something kept for future use or retained from present use to be used for another purpose. A reserve can also be something in the mind withheld from disclosure, that is now revealed.

The Triumphant Reserve!

What the Lord showed me on May 31, 2008 was His Triumphant Reserve that would be called up for future Kingdom purposes. He showed me that many would begin to move out of the enemy's camp of religion. He also showed me that many would refuse to leave their religious structures. When He began to gather His new reserve together, it was as if many were not attracted by this new movement and remained steadfast in the old place of worship and religious rule that had become comfortable in their life. He showed me how others were aligning around race and gender as opposed to mission call and gifting. However, He showed me how this fiery river of God's people would become the movement of the future. This would be the group that would destroy the works of the enemy in days ahead!

Then He showed me **HIGH PLACES**. Each state in America had high places that had developed through the years from idolatrous worship and wrong sacrifice. High places are actually worship altars. These were altars that had been built by the enemy and positioned strategically throughout the land. I saw how the sacrifices on these altars were empowering and keeping an atmosphere held captive by ruling hosts.

Next, the Lord showed me the **ATMOSPHERE**. In this vision He showed me different layers of the atmosphere in relationship to His presence versus the demonic spiritual rule in that particular area or region. (Some areas had already been taken over, and darkness was actually ruling those areas.) The enemy had 10 ruling centers already developed within the United States. These were positioned strategically throughout the land. They were like communication centers that communicated to lesser substations from state to state to state. Then He showed me the communication systems between these centers. I saw how one sacrifice empowered one dimension of an evil presence, and then that presence would communicate to another center as they networked together their plan of control. (I could go into great detail here, but I will wait for another time to do this. Matter of fact, I believe it would be unwise to share everything I saw.)

The Lord then showed me the **COVENANT ROOTS** that He had in this nation. He actually showed me the level of nurturing that was still grafted to His covenant root that He had developed from Abraham's obedience. He showed me how this nation had first been nurtured by that root, but now lifelines from the root system had withered. Actually, some of the lifelines in parts of this nation had dried up and the root system of that part of the nation had changed and a different root structure had formed. He showed me how some roots were covered over by a mossy, evil slime that could be removed. He showed me states that had never allowed a covenant root to go down in their land. He showed me broken covenants that would have to be mended before roots could grow fruit for the future.

He then showed me our **CONFLICT BETWEEN THE ROOT SYSTEMS**. These conflicts in the next several years would determine what sort of fruit would be brought forth in this nation. He showed me that the conflicts would multiply and intensify. I actually saw "orchards of contention." The interesting portion of this vision was that different people groups in each orchard created a different type of fruit than had been tasted of in past seasons. The only thing I could relate it to biblically was the church that came out of Antioch. The Antioch church was an international church that came about for Kingdom advancement for that season in history.

Next, He showed me how the **COMMUNICATION SYSTEM** in the

United States was linked with systems internationally, and how a new form of global communications was beginning in the demonic world. This communication would control financial and legal structures. All of these structures had a ruling voice that was set against the God of Israel. Therefore, I knew that during these next seven years, beginning in 2008, that Israel would experience much warfare. Interestingly, it was during this time I sent my son, Daniel, and his wife, Amber, to live there.

However, He also showed me His remnant buildings that the LORD Himself was erecting. These looked like fiery, vibrant castles strategically developed and placed in the earth. Not every state had one of these fiery centers. I asked the Lord what this was, and He said, *"**There are my FREEDOM OUTPOSTS for the future.**"* His Triumphant Reserve then connected with the centers. When they did, they went in one way and came out seven times brighter and stronger.

I saw 23 states in America that had covenant roots. Many states had Freedom Outposts. But He then showed me how other outposts needed to form in some places. Where the spiritual atmosphere was not yet conducive to freedom, I saw how outposts could begin to form, and new types of warfare that would have to be developed by this triumphant people to regain new portions of the land.

During this four-hour visitation, He actually showed me how prayer strategies from the last season would not be effective in this season. Nazareth and Capernaum are good examples of this from Jesus' day. I thought of how the Lord told the disciples, *"These will not come out except through prayer and fasting."* Of course, now I believe what He was showing me was the **APOSTOLIC CHURCH ARISING** and **APOSTOLIC CENTERS FORMING** for a shift in a worship war in the earth realm. The vision continued by Him showing me 153 nations that would align with Israel and become sheep nations for the future. I then saw new calls being extended from heaven and angels bringing those calls into the earth. The intercession and travail of today are opening the Gates of Heaven for these calls to come to the appropriate ones that will lead in this hour. Next, He showed me His new leadership. This was not a leadership of just the young generation, but **realigned generations**; it was as if David's Mighty Army for this hour was being chosen in a **three-fold generational alignment**. When they aligned, their hearts became one with His and the strength to overcome was released.

Apostolic Centers Represent the Kingdom!

Now I see these Freedom Outposts have become apostolic centers for the future. Apostolic centers are different from mega-churches. These are the key glory hubs where war and triumphant strategies will be released to advance the Church in days ahead. These are Kingdom centers. There is a big difference between an apostolic center and normal church fellowship gathering.

Dr. Elmer Towns is presently writing a book, *Ten of the Largest Church Ministries Influencing the World*. In this book he shares about Glory of Zion International Ministries. Glory of Zion, located in the Global Spheres Center in Corinth, Texas. Here is some of what he shares:

> *Glory of Zion International uses the internet to fulfill the Great Commission to reach, teach, baptize, and train people, worldwide. Some ask if online interaction can be a church if people are not gathered in one place. Is it a denomination? Or a church*

planting agency? Chuck D. Pierce, president and prophetic leader of Glory of Zion International was assigned to "align" God's "scattered sheep" from around the world. His description of "aligned members" is a noun for "church membership" used by churches. He gathers all kinds of believers from all different places and cultures of the world.

Pierce took leadership of a small local church in Denton, TX, and taught "core values" concerning the foundation of the Church and the first principles of the Word of God, including Israel. This became the rallying cry in a movement that has now become an international online church. Some describe it as a Google denomination or a Google church. Dr. Pierce describes it as God realigning the Body of Christ to bring us into His call of One New Man, Jew and Gentile, in latter days (Eph. 2:14-16).

Glory of Zion is made up of "aligned" members from home churches (begun by the movement) of approximately 1,200 believers from North Texas, and then approximately 30,000 individual believers from all over the world. There are also Businesses of Zion (commercial) and Churches of Zion (pre-existing churches that have aligned and are tied together by regular internet connection). Chuck visits his "flock" through world-wide conferences where individuals and groups come together for instruction, fellowship, motivation, and re-enforcement of purpose. Once every four to six weeks the staff spends a week praying for each person that is aligned with the ministry.

I asked Chuck Pierce why he began an online church. He

answered, "I had always used the internet and was beginning to move into a wider communication structure with other social media. I had a desire to develop a world-wide prayer movement. I didn't originally think of developing an online church."

Pierce thought deeply and explained, "The idea of an online church began during the first decade of this millennium when the Lord spoke to me, 'Gather the scattered sheep.' That was the word from God that He wanted me to focus on His 'scattered sheep' around the world. My question was, how can I do it? So, God said to me, 'Use the communication system that you are now using, use the internet and social media to gather my sheep.'"

Pierce said, "I didn't just want to broadcast a message to the 'scattered sheep,' I needed a relationship with them to effectively minister to them. God was instructing me to form a spiritual relationship that would attach them to the Lord and to one another, so they could grow in Christ."

When Pierce was asked "Who are these scattered sheep?", he answered, "These are people who have left the traditional church for many reasons, yet they still had a tender heart toward God and want to worship God." He began his online church by asking them to align with him in a relationship, so they could receive a unique message about the body of Christ for them through him.

Building an Apostolic Prototype

Even though we have been gathering quite an army through using man's tool of the internet, the Lord had one more step for us to create a prototype for the next season. As I said earlier, it's hard to build until you see how God is building from heaven. In 2011, we had met our capacity in the third phase of this ministry. We were gathering in an office center and had rented 100,000 square feet to do all the Lord asked us to do. This included gathering a church of 800, teaching the Issachar School, and attempting to do community activities. The rent continued to escalate on this prime office space. Therefore, I knew we needed to make a shift. We began to seek the Lord for wisdom and direction. Ten years prior, when Boeing had vacated their 268,000 square foot facility in Corinth that was used to make cockpits, they approached us about purchasing the facility. However, the price was enormous.

As I sought the Lord, I had a dream over what the place He had for us would look like. He showed me a property with a small lake on it. I will not go into further detail, but the dream showed how this property connected my past with my future. After I had this dream, I was once again contacted by the people still representing this Boeing property -- now 10 years later. The price had dropped enormously on the building that had sat vacant and desolate over those years. Through incredibly supernatural events, the Lord had us purchase the facility for 1/3 of the original asking price ten years prior. Little did I know that the Lord would begin to build a prototype for the future. I cannot begin to tell you all the process we have gone through over these last eight years. However, we are on the verge of restoring all 41 acres, including the 268,000 square foot facility. During this time, I have learned that God is building a new prototype in days ahead called "apostolic centers."

Church Versus Apostolic Center

Churches and apostolic centers have many things in common – they are both a place to gather and fellowship. But there are differences. I believe the early Church had to learn to gather both in homes and in key places to represent apostolic authority as they developed God's prototype that first 70 years. Both are places where you build for the future. To build actually means to add sons and daughters from generation to generation. Both are places where generations must align. Isaiah 59:21 is a key verse to better understand when God is doing a new thing or bringing us into a new era: *"'As for me, this is my covenant with them,' says the Lord. 'My Spirit, who is on you, will not depart from you, and my words that I have put in your mouth will always be on your lips, on the lips of your children and on the lips of their descendants—from this time on and forever,' says the Lord."* (NKJV) Three generations must prophesy God's destiny together for the glory shift to occur.

However, apostolic centers have some different characteristics than just a normal church gathering. They are one of the central places of activity for a community. This is how transformation occurs in a region. When we first began to develop what is now called the Global Spheres Center, the relationship between us and the community was strained. What had brought in a great amount of taxes was now a non-profit work zoned as a spiritual center. Three years elapsed before we came into a good community relationship. Now, the Global Spheres Center is where most events for the four surrounding cities take place. Through our gatherings, we fill the hotels and bring more finances into the city and community than the prior industry representation ever accomplished.

From a spiritual standpoint, an apostolic center becomes a place where we ascend in worship and create a prophetic portal. This allows revelation to flow back and forth from heaven into a corporate people that are represented in approximately 180 nations worldwide. This center has a great travailing remnant that is aligned throughout the world and teaches prevailing Kingdom principles that show people how to be in the world but not of it. An apostolic center like this gains Kingdom strategies over how to affect territories and nations. As Yeshua said, we must seek the Kingdom first.

Therefore, apostolic centers are not merely trying to establish the sheep, but to advance the sheep into the future. An apostolic center represents the true meaning of the word apostle – they send forth people on missions throughout the world. We have a passion to find out how to break through into regions that have never broken through and to establish people to rise up in the Spirit of God in those regions. This apostolic center is being prepared to host a move of God. As many key leaders are saying, we are on the verge of a Third Great Awakening. In days ahead, apostolic centers will be used to host that awakening and be a place where the move of God can be established.

As you will read in subsequent chapters from Robert Heidler, an apostolic center is a place to experiment with the gifts of God until we become mature in our faith.

Endnotes

1   Chuck D. Pierce and Rebecca Wagner Sytsema, *The Future War of the Church*, (Regal Books, 2001, 2007); Chuck D. Pierce, *God's Unfolding Battle Plan*, (Chosen Books, 2007); Chuck D. Pierce, *A Time to Triumph*, (Chosen Books, 2016).

2   Chuck D. Pierce with Rebecca Wagner Sytsema, *The Spiritual Warfare Handbook*, (Chosen Books, 2000, 2004, 2005, 2016).

3   Dutch Sheets and Chuck Pierce, *Releasing the Prophetic Destiny of a Nation*, (Destiny Image, 2005).

3

Advancing in the War Ahead!

War is the *"grace to fight."* When the Lord calls us to war, He gives us the grace to triumph. God never calls His children to do anything without the grace that is necessary to fulfill His purpose. Therefore, in the midst of war, there is grace. One of the key chapters that I have written is in *A Time to Triumph: How to Win the War Ahead*[1]. The name of that chapter is "Why Christians Must Learn to War." We are called to protect our vineyard. My greatest concern for the Church today is, *"Will a new generation rise up and war for all the promises that have been redeemed or paid for by the Blood of the Lord Jesus Christ?"*

Christians must learn why it's imperative that we fight and overturn the plans of the enemy. Learning to war comes easier to some than to others. To those who grew up in relative peace and comfort, it may come hardest of all. Why war? Why is war necessary? Why can't people live in harmony? These are the questions we ask our parents when we are first exposed to conflict, through the media. We ask the questions of our history teachers when we are learning the events that brought us to the present. Most importantly, we ask God, *"If you are a loving God, why do war and destruction occur?"*

The short answer is that there are two kingdoms in conflict. Satan's demonic angels roam the earth trying to keep his kingdom in place. We are in God's Army of Warriors. The Lord has already defeated Satan and all his dominions, powers, and principalities. However, we are called to enforce that defeat. If we do not heed His call, then the enemy will step in and rule in our stead. We are called to possess, secure, and protect our inheritance. We must remember that the earth is the Lord's and the fullness thereof!

As the Holy Spirit moves us toward becoming more Christ-like, the methodology of an old season will not propel us into the future. We need something new and fresh. We need a new glory. This is one of the wiles of the enemy - to hold us captive in the last manifestation of God. Therefore, we live in the past rather than move into the best that is ahead for our lives. This is how religious spirits operate.

A Season of War!

We are living in conflicting and conflicted times. Many times, the shifts we make are not our willful choices but a result from the wars of the season. We would have loved to see something go one way, but atmospheric shifts, conflicts of opinions, conflicts of philosophies, and conflicts of emotions caused things to go a different direction. James said that we war because we have cravings and desires in us that cannot be satisfied. Many times, these desires hold us in wilderness places. We are meant to cross over into prosperity, but we choose to have our way in a situation, instead of submitting to the will of God. We are in a great warfare over a three-fold cord controlled by Satan's kingdom consisting of: poverty, infirmity, and religion.

We are now living in times of war. This war is very different than the declared times of World War I and II. There seems to be world conflict, and no one is immune from the effects. I believe this is because we live in a fourth dimension that has only existed in recent years: social media, internet, instantaneous communication worldwide. Even in a war season, God's army has different rules that we must play by. We must understand time, timing, and God-given missions that lead to triumph. Each year, I attempt to seek the Lord to gain revelation that causes us to better perceive what the voice of God would love to speak through His people. We are His voice in the earth in every generation and must remain His voice crying in the wilderness. Our decrees open the way for the Lord to come into our season. Once we decree a thing, we then watch to see God's will manifest. This season of war is becoming very real to most of us now and actually is historic in a sense. We are now pressing into the next season. The new wineskin of the Church should now be formed to express victory in the next season.

Alain Caron has masterfully developed a manual to understand Kingdom as we advance into the season ahead. *Apostolic Expansion: The Kingdom War for Territorial Gains*[2] is a must book for any leader, intercessor, or warrior to have and dissect. I believe Alain takes us further into a Kingdom understanding than any book I have seen recently. He then moves us through the process of expansion, harvest, and rest. The final portion of the book anchors us into the redemptive plan linked to a territory and gives us an urgency for territorial gains. The Spirit of God is now developing centers where a Kingdom display and performance can occur. The Lord not only declares His Word, but He performs His Word and manifests His glory. These centers are prototypes of what Heaven is displaying for the earth to see.

Both Alain, as well as Robert Heidler and myself, have written books that help us understand the apostolic church as an apostolic center, *Apostolic Centers: Shifting the Church, Transforming the World* and *The Apostolic Church*

A TRIUMPHANT KINGDOM

Arising³, respectively.

A Recent Visit to Pearl Harbor

We are entering into three accelerated years of conflict. In the mist of the worldwide conflict, we will see authority structures and economic structures changing, and power demonstrations occurring. China and Russia will both be at the forefront of stirring up much of the conflict worldwide. The United States will continue to stand for democracy. However, in the midst of her stand there will be many wars over the freedoms we have known over the last 400 years.

One of our sons, Isaac Pierce, married Celestine Patu, the lead dancer for Island Breeze on the island of Kona, Hawaii. Yearly our families attempt to be together whether here at one of our key events or on the Big Island of Hawaii. On our last visit, Pam and I both knew we needed to fly through Honolulu and go to Pearl Harbor. The Lord impressed us separately of the historical importance of doing this. When we visited Pearl Harbor, I noticed the events leading up to the surprise bombing of this American port and key watchtower in the Pacific. America had entered into troubled times through 1929-1941. Here are the events:

- 1929 - The American stock market crashes, triggering the Great Depression.
- 1931-33 - Japan seizes Manchuria and creates the puppet state of Manchukuo. Condemned for invading Manchuria, Japan quits the League of Nations. The military solidifies control over the government in Tokyo.

Advancing in the War Ahead!

- 1937 - Japan launches an undeclared war against China. The Japanese sink the gunboat USS Panay near Nanking, increasing tension between the U.S. and Japan.
- 1938 - Germany annexes Austria; Britain and France do not interfere. Japan takes notice.
- 1939 - Germany invades Poland, igniting World War II in Europe.
- 1940 - Japanese troops occupy Indochina. Japan signs the Tri-Partite Pact with Germany and Italy, creating the Tokyo-Rome-Berlin Axis.
- 1941 - The U.S. seizes Japanese and Chinese financial assets and cuts off oil exports to Japan.

Usually, a worldwide crisis is linked to provision, or the lack thereof. What fueled this crisis was a lust for power. The world economic crisis ushered in the Great Depression. This caused America to turn inward. Germany, Italy, and Japan were doing the opposite - they were seeking to expand their rule. The rise of Nazism in Germany, Fascism in Italy, and Militarism in Japan led to global destabilization and threatened the democracy of the world. A stock market crash sent the United States into economic depression. Military actions by the Japanese in China, the Italians in Ethiopia, and the Germans in Poland sowed the seeds of global war. I have recently visited all of those key battle fields.

In response to Japanese aggression in Asia, the United States imposed economic embargos and deployed its Pacific Fleet to Pearl Harbor. Commercial Attaché Frank S. Williams wrote, "*Perhaps the phase of our order which struck the deepest into the sensibilities of the Japanese was that at last the United States has shown this country that it is no longer bluffing."*[4] However, there was a passivity that America had embraced which resulted in us not heeding key watchman warnings. This allowed the worst attack in American history to that date upon our ability to war and move into the future.

As Pam and I compared notes and sought the Lord, what we both saw was a very similar pattern that is occurring today. Instead of Japan, Germany, and Italy, it is now China, Russia, and the Middle East. Pam, who grew up in an Air Force family, started thinking from a military mindset. I started thinking from a spiritual apostolic warfare mindset. I started crying out to the Lord to continue to raise up His remnant people who could go to war in the spiritual realm to realign the structures that I mentioned earlier: authorities, economics, and demonstrative power. The Lord began to give me a list of the apostolic prophetic rule that must be established. I will discuss that a bit later.

Heaven and Earth Must Align

In many books I have written, I've discussed the three heavens, and heaven and earth aligning. This is really how the Lord taught His disciples to pray – by using a great model prayer which we know as the Lord's prayer (on earth as it is in heaven). **The government of heaven must enter our atmosphere, align with the government of God in the earth and liberate the armies of God and the land!** Joshua 5 is one of the best examples of heaven and earth realigning and the Lord intervening on behalf of the promise of the people. Once Israel had entered the Promised Land, they were in the right place for supernatural intervention from heaven. Upon leaving Egypt 40 years prior, the Lord had promised that if the people would move by faith, angelic help would come. Finally, after 40 years, God sent an angel to assist them in the war ahead. This occurred after Israel did a prophetic act of circumcising the next generation. Circumcision was a sign of the covenant that God had with this peculiar people. None of the generation that had been in the wilderness had been circumcised, and this prophetic act caused the atmosphere of the entire camp to change. The reproach of unbelief that the people had been carrying for 40 years was rolled away. The next thing that happened was the daily provision that had been coming ceased. Things were changing rapidly. Ahead of them was Jericho, the most invincible city of all the Promised Land.

While Joshua was mediating on the strategy to advance, a man appeared and stood opposite him with his sword drawn. Joshua asked, "Are you for us or for our adversaries?" He answered, "No, I have come now as Captain of the Army of the Lord." Upon his arrival he commanded Joshua to remove the sandals he had been wearing from the last season and set him apart and commissioned him for the task ahead. When we see the open window for change and victory above us, we must submit to God's new order that He is forming and advance as He commands. His order will produce breakthrough.

The Plumb Line of Heaven Touches Earth!

Prophets are interesting creatures. They see into heavenly realms the demonstrations of what will eventually occur in the natural. Zechariah saw a plumb line coming down from heaven. This is the day when the Lord is dropping His plumb line into the earth over cities and territories and nations. If you have any background in building, you know that when a plumb line is released, all your framework must align with it.

A plumb line is a line with a weight on the end that is directed toward the center of gravity. This causes whatever is being erected to come into vertical alignment. When the restorative prophet Zechariah saw the plumb line, he saw the following:

- A new and revised building plan for the future.
- Revelation producing supernatural guidance that would cause one vision to fully manifest.
- Restoration from the past. After the people of God had been in captivity 70 years, Zechariah saw God's people with a new identity and authority.
- A restorative process that would bring God's plan for His covenant people into completion. This would break the power of postponement of past blessings.
- A new grace that would shout down the mountains that had been their obstacles of the past.
- Multiplied restoration – a double return for their loss!
- Most importantly, a full alignment with covenant blessings for the future.

Heaven wants us to see God's plumb line made up of the words and prayers of the saints from the last season that never came to completion. His word in this era is now beginning to manifest.

A Time to Plow

"Behold, the days are coming," says the Lord, "When the plowman shall overtake the reaper, and the treader of grapes him who sows seed; the mountains

shall drip with sweet wine, and all the hills shall flow with it." (Amos 9:13, NKJV)

One of the key passages to understand today is Amos 9. This chapter is critical to our future. David created a prototype that had never been seen on the earth. Under the Law, David's Tabernacle was actually illegal, but God gave the prototype! The Lord provided a supernatural release and glory for His Ark to move from one season into its position for the next. When Amos prophesied this, he said that the Tabernacle of David would be restored. For the early church to advance in confusing times, they had to refer to Amos' prophecy. The book of Revelation is about the Tabernacle of David being restored. We are now living in this time!

Recently, in Houston, I shared what the Lord had shown me for the year ahead. I asked Him specifically what His word was for 2019 and He said these words to me **"PLOW THROUGH IT!"** I shared this when Lora Allison was in the meeting. I have known Lora for many, many years, but I forgot that she had written about plowing. When I finished speaking, she said, "Do you remember the book I wrote several decades ago about the plowmen overtaking the reapers?" I said, "Vaguely, I remember part of it." She promptly said, "The Lord instructed me to redo that book for today!" I grabbed the opportunity to go back through the revelation that the Lord had given her. *The Plowmen Shall Overtake the Reaper*[5] is the book for this hour! I have not read anything that better represents the decade ahead. If I could recommend one book to read other than the Bible, I would say to read this. There are great blessings that are coming quickly, as we allow God to bring down His plumb line and co-labor with Him to build His plan in the earth for the future.

Prophetic seeds that have been sown and declared in your region should be plowed up! The Lord has put us into a plowing season. Most importantly, He has given us this incredible tool to equip us. The prophetic seeds that didn't come up in one season should be declared and planted again. I see teams of plowmen being connected together. Many of us have received revelation but tried to plow alone. However, if we connect and plow together, the harvest of God in a region will be gathered. There is a specific timing we must be in if we want to reap the harvest. That's why God is speaking to His Church about this passage of scripture. This is a key time for alignment. Lora addresses not only the seed and the sower, but how we must plow together in days ahead and not sow in vain.

Apostolic/Prophetic Rule Must Be Established in a New Way

As the apostolic Church matures and advances the Kingdom of God in the earth, apostolic/prophetic rule will be established in territories. Here are six key points that we must understand as we move forward in this new era:

- *Know your field and sphere.* As I shared earlier, faith works in place and time. In 2 Corinthians 10, Paul talks about fields, or spheres. We each have key fields and spheres that we can war and triumph within.
- *Mobilize the armies.* Know who is warring with you for the King's rule.
- *Strategically know your redemptive "thin" places.* When Rose Sambrook from Northern Ireland came to speak at one of our gatherings, she shared how in Ireland they talk about "thin places." These are the places where the Spirit of God has come,

and heaven and earth have become very close. These places have key altars that need to be re-fired for today. We must know where these altars are in our field or spheres. If there are no thin places in our sphere then we must find where the Lord wants to come and create a thin place, or portal, between heaven and earth.

- ◆ ***Define the high places.*** Within our spheres and field, we also have high places. These are places where the enemy has erected his rule. These are the places contending for our worship.
- ◆ ***Sanctify the land.*** When we commit iniquitous sins and defilement of the land occurs, we must sanctify the land. The land mourns until we have reconciled it back to God, the One who made it. The earth is the Lord's and the fullness thereof (Ps. 24:1).
- ◆ ***Establish new glory altars.*** *High Places and Ruling Demonic Centers Must Fall!*

There are many high places erected by the enemy throughout the nations. These are the result of the worship war going on in each territory of the earth. Worship occurs around the one whose throne has been established. We are made to worship; therefore, if we pay homage to the enemy, he will control the atmosphere. The entire territory then falls under the darkness of his presence, and demonic hosts redirect those in that territory away from God's plan of fullness, peace, joy, and abundance.

Build a New Glory Altar

All through the Word of God new altars had to be built. How do we do this? We must find the places where religion and government have met and made wrong choices and bind the strongman (Mt. 12). We must overthrow the defilement of the last altar (2 Chron 34:4; John 2:14; Rev. 2:13). Contend for His name to be established and the identity of that name at the gates (Dt. 28:10). Let worship ascend and watch His glory come down (John 4, Acts 4-11). Welcome a new move of His spirit (Acts-Ephesians).

The Time of Harvest is Now!

Biblically, God's goal for us is the harvest. We see this all the way through the Bible. God wants our barns to be filled with plenty and for our vats to overflow. He wants us to experience the fullness of His promised blessings. That's what harvest means. Harvest is what we've been working and praying for. It's the promise that God has held out before us, the promise that we have been pressing into. The time does come when we will receive the harvest. Harvest is not "pie in the sky by and by," but the reality of the promise coming into our experience. God not only wants us to harvest in the natural realm, but also to see a harvest of righteousness. He wants us to experience a harvest of souls. But there is a time for harvest. Psalm 1 tells us that God wants us to be like a flourishing tree that brings forth its fruit in its season. Ecclesiastes 3 tells us there is a time and a season for everything. There is a time to plant seeds, and there is also a time to reap the harvest.

We must be in God's timing. God wants us to have an abundant harvest, but if we aren't in the right time and season, we will not reap it. Too often, the Church goes out to harvest in the wrong season and instead of getting grain, it just gets snowed on. If you're not in the right season, you won't get a harvest. That's a basic principle.

God Has Established Many Laws

One of the most familiar is the law of the harvest, which says that a person will reap what he or she sows. That's a description of how the universe operates and is like the law of gravity. If you want to have a bountiful harvest, you must first sow your seed. When you understand the law of the harvest, you are enabled to prosper. A law is really just a picture of reality. It's a description of how things work. For example, the law of gravity is a description of how objects behave on planet Earth. On this planet, when you let go of an object, it falls. That's the law of gravity.

Satan uses times and laws to stop God's people from advancing and manifesting His grace and power. Daniel 7:25 says that Satan tries to wear down our minds, or ways of thinking, to capture us and consequently capture the blessings and promises God intended for us. Once we agree, or fall prey to Satan's ways, we begin to decrease rather than increase. The enemy's plan of devastation takes effect, and we begin to lose the war of resisting.

When this happens, we move from operating in the laws of prosperity and begin to embrace poverty. Satan overtakes our minds with a flood of thoughts that starts this reversal. Instead of thinking prosperity and meditating on the covenant that God has with us, we develop a poverty mindset.

We must remain alert to what is happening in our field, or the enemy will attempt to get his hands on what belongs to us. When we grow passive and are not aware of the enemy's scheme to rob our supplies and assets, he maneuvers and manipulates his way into the storehouses meant for us. When the enemy gains an upper hand over our inheritance, we lose our stewardship and our ability to multiply. When we fail to capitalize on the opportunity to bring in our harvest, he steals the field.

Plant, Watch and Gather!

We can plant, watch our crops grow and have breakthrough, but if we do not take the opportunity to gather and steward the spoils, a strategy of poverty will begin to develop against us. Remember the story of Gideon. Every year at harvest times, for seven years, the Midianites would let Israel grow the harvest and then come to steal, rob, and plunder. When we increase without developing storehouses to contain our spoils, we eventually lose the spoils, and poverty begins to work.

Refusing to become what God created and destined you to be causes poverty to work in your life. Not believing that the Lord can branch you into the fullness of His plan is just as bad as refusing to become what He intended and created you to become. Poverty thinking is not just experiencing lack, but also having a fear that you will lack. When you conform to your circumstances or come into agreement with the blueprint of the world, the prince of this world will use you until he has fully captured your strength for his purpose.

Most of us do not understand harvest time. Because of our complex lives, we are far removed from the actual production of our food supplies and the source of our provision. The harvest was significant (see Gen. 8:22; 45:6). Events were reckoned from harvests (see Gen. 30:14; Josh. 3:15; Judg. 15:1; Ruth 1:22; 2:23; 1 Sam. 6:13; 2 Sam. 21:9; 23:13). For instance, take the Pentecost Feast which represents:

- A season of gathering (see Zech. 8).
- A season of judgment (see Jer. 51:33; Joel 3:13; Rev 14:15)
- A season of grace (see Jer. 8:20)
- A time for the good news to be heard (see Matt. 9:37-38; John 4:35)
- An end of a season and beginning of a new season of provision (see Mt. 13:39)

His Word is built around harvest. This harvest includes both physical as well as spiritual blessings. We must know our moment. Another unction the Lord gave me for all of us was, "Tell My people not to miss their moment!" It is vital for our future. I often sense that we are a people who miss much of what we should see. I believe the Lord is saying, "Look again!" He wants us to see beyond—to see in ways we have not seen and see what He has prepared for us. To see beyond where we presently see, both spiritually and physically, we must become aware that God IS opening up our path ahead. (Psalm 21)

Angelic Assistance is on the Way

God has a government. He is Lord Sabaoth, "The God of Hosts." He has an army in heaven and He aligns that Host with His Kingdom army in the earth. When we are moving in God's glory, angelic visitation occurs. In December 2017, I was chosen by the Lord for an angelic visitation. The first place I ever shared this visitation was at a regional gathering hosted by Apostle Tim Sheets. We must co-labor with the Host of Heaven when we are moving in the glory realm in the earth. We are the army of earth. The Host of Heaven interacts with us to bring His victory into the earth realm.

The angel from my visitation was peering into the Harvest throughout the earth. I entered into what he was seeing, but neither space nor time permits to share all of it here. When I asked him what his name was, he said, **"I am the Angel of War over God's Covenant Harvest Plan."** He revealed to me the harvest shift that we would enter, and how this is a time for us to break out of conventional ways of thinking. We must make a "harvest shift" and be led through the "gate of harvest increase." There will be a great hardening, separation, and then a sharpening! This will draw out the army-order of the present Body…and be the *first harvest training!* This angel took me through several other steps of training that we will go through in the future.

- Grace will be sovereignly extended for wrong alignments in past covenants…. This will be the *second harvest training! (Hagars, Ishmaels, Brothers and Sisters who persecuted you, Esaus, Marks!)*
- Saints' eyes will be opened to the carrion-scavengers which have ravished their covenant plan! This will be the *third harvest training!* (Your bloodline and mission)
- New *angelic councils* will be forming and assigned to territories. These teams will meet with Apostolic-Prophetic Councils in the earth realm, to give strategies for advancement. This will be the *fourth harvest training!*
- The Desire of Nations will begin to reveal Himself! Public decrees will be heard from nation's civil leaders which will call entire territories and peoples into awakening…. This will be the *fifth harvest training!*
- God's People will be sorted by their faithfulness in gleaning.

> This will give them REAPING Access... This will be the *sixth harvest training!* The Territorial Threshing Floors for the Harvest will be revealed! New calls to harvesters will be extended.... This will be the *seventh harvest training!*

As the God of Hosts, the Lord has angels and saints coming together to advance the Kingdom. We have entered a season of heightened angelic visitation. Already we are probably visited by more angels than we know.

In *The New Era of Glory: Stepping Into God's Accelerated Season of Outpouring and Breakthrough!*[6], Apostle Tim Sheets explains the glory war ahead and gives us a road map for the future. His book takes us beyond our present understanding, into revelation for a new era. Revelation 4:1-2 says, *"After these things I looked, and behold, a door standing open in heaven. And the first voice which I heard was like a trumpet speaking with me, saying, 'Come up here, and I will show you things which must take place after this.' Immediately I was in the Spirit; and behold, a throne set in heaven, and One sat on the throne."* The door that God is opening is in the heavenly realm. He is aligning that door over us in the earth realm which then causes angelic help to come. This opens the door to our future. This is exactly what we are experiencing in this new season. Heavenly portals are being opened and God's angelic host is flooding into our atmosphere.

The Spirit of God is saying, *"Go forth by My Spirit with My help ... with My ministering angelic host and do the war ahead."* We have entered a season when we will need the angels to interact with us as never before. Angelic visitation is an important concept to understand once the portal of glory has been established connecting heaven and earth. I have seen angels only a few times, but I do recognize their presence. I believe this is a type of discernment that comes through worshiping and knowing the glory of God and how His presence manifests around us. Imagine the angels showing up to announce in the fields near Bethlehem that the glory of God had come to earth! Although angels often precede God's glory, they also follow after it.

Keep Praying, Knocking and Seeking!

There is a great war over establishing God's Kingdom plan in the earth realm. Because of what we are warring against, we must have an effective prayer strategy. In the late 1970s, the Lord began to move in me to renew and energize my prayer life. I found myself staying up late and praying. God gave me actual prayer assignments. He had me pray for individuals, for my Sunday School class, for our church, for my pastor, and for the church staff. I prayed for the company where I worked. I prayed for my family. I simply was enjoying communicating with the Lord and watching Him work.

One night after I had my prayer time, I went to bed. At 2:00 AM, I was awakened, and our dog was growling and getting into the bed with us. My wife, Pam, was awakened and startled as well. I felt a presence in our room. Pam described this presence as a slimy green vapor—it was at the end of our bed. I stood up on our bed and commanded this presence to leave our house. I knew that enemy was angry over my prayer life becoming active. This evil force was hoping to deter me from getting to know the Lord better. It was as if he was attempting to produce fear in me so I would stop praying. He knew that if I kept seeking the Lord with all my heart, I would eventually be free and able to recognize and confront him in new ways, to defeat his purposes.

We must never let the enemy create fear in us, nor be afraid of understanding the enemy's schemes, character, and ways. In ***Next Level Spiritual Warfare: Advanced Strategies for Defeating the Enemy***,[7] Dr. Venner Alston provides foundational principles that will help you and others become more effective in praying and experiencing answers to your prayers. Like few others, this resource will help you rise up and turn back the battle at the gates.

The Council Room of the Lord: Accessing the Power of God

Another book that is key for the moment in which we live is Barbara Wentroble's, *The Council Room of the Lord: Accessing the Power of God*[8]. Any blood-bought believer can enter the "Council Room" of God. I love this small book that is power packed with keys to accessing what we need to triumph on a daily basis.

In the new covenant dispensation, the enemy is blocked from entering into the Throne Room. However, YOU HAVE ACCESS! The access will release power that will cause the enemy to flee! 1 Corinthians 2:6-9 talks about God's secret plan and wisdom that did not originate from this present age, but before the ages, to bring us into glory. No matter how established you are, there will be new beginnings in your life, ministry, and spheres of authority. We, the Body of Christ, must **manifest who we are and who we represent!** The Lord is forming a new order in the earth realm from His Council Room. ***This is a time to:***

- ◆ *Gain ACCESS to your GARDEN!* That was the first premise of boundaries. Within our new boundaries are the manifestations of glory and the communion of our future.
- ◆ *Gain ACCESS to the Kingdom of God!* We will under-

stand the Kingdom of God within us and demonstrate Kingdom-power within our sphere.

- ◆ *Gain ACCESS to the blessings of Abraham's covenant and align with Israel - God's First Nation!*
- ◆ *Gain ACCESS to mysteries held in His Word!* There must be a revival of the Word of God in the Body of Christ. (Father gave Torah to Israel and then the Son demonstrated His HEART and MIND to us.)
- ◆ *Gain ACCESS to a new timing, linked with harvest!*
- ◆ *Gain ACCESS to the ark* and understand the *procession of Glory* in our region!
- ◆ *Gain ACCESS to understanding the Government of God in Heaven and Earth.* This will mobilize an army for war!
- ◆ *Gain ACCESS to new sound that will produce movement. Judah goes first!* We are poised to gain ACCESS to *NEW SONGS* that will break old cycles!
- ◆ *Gain ACCESS to the understanding of God's order in our land!*

You Have Unprecedented Access

Go boldly into His throne room! He is waiting. Be like Esther and ask for favor. Be like Joseph and wear a new mantle of favor wherever you are located. Favor, even in confinement, will open a new door of entry. Ask the Lord what "one thing" you need to do to unlock your next phase. Jesus had to be baptized by John. Let your right-standing come forth. The Lord is longing to crown you with righteousness. Do not allow the accuser's condemning

Advancing in the War Ahead!

voice to stop you from wearing that crown. Dominion comes when we wear the crown (Ps. 9). We are the righteousness of God in Christ Jesus, but you must wear the crown of that righteousness. Our righteousness must become experiential. Stand in your righteousness. Set your face to obey and to do what will keep you in right standing so that the enemy can't accuse you later for not doing something you should have done. Ask the Lord to reform the foundation for your standing. You may have to make a shift because the foundation you stood on in the past season is too shaky for you to stand on in the next season. Allow the Lord to solidify your stance so you walk in the fullness of what He will cause to blossom.

Do not let *joy robbers* stop you from experiencing God's best. The Spirit of God will see to it that you celebrate. If you feel like your celebration is dwindling, just ask Him to release an anointing of *gladness*. This will sanctify you and cause you to press past that old season. Stop and hear the trees clap their hands. When you hear the wind blowing in the mulberry trees, you will receive a new strategy to come from behind and overtake the enemy that has blockaded your path. Watch where the winds blow. Catch the wind. You can catch up quickly. Move into that new place of victory. You will surprise the enemy. The Lord is saying, "I will give you cautions well in advance so you can shift the direction of your path."

Ask for your root system to be reformed and that the roots of righteousness deep in you would be watered and begin to flourish. Ask the Lord to bring you past milk. Begin to digest the *protein* the Lord is giving you at this time. Declare that you will step through the gate of life into a new type of nourishment. Go out of your old place with joy, delight, and happiness. Ask for a realignment of your heart-desires with His heart-desires. Then ask the Lord to allow you to hear the stillness of the heavens. In the midst of your chaos, ask Him to let you hear the stillness of His shadow. Ask Him to let you hear sounds you have not heard. Tell Him you are listening and let Him circulate the atmosphere of heaven around you. Ask Him to bring and activate your atmospheric change. Let the cares of the day slip away so you hear the will of heaven. Don't go out in your own strength. Wait for the pulsating heart of God to propel forth the blood in your heart. Do not contend over how others are moving forward. Rid yourself of anxiety and stop questioning how you will ever get everything done to advance into your best in days ahead.

Doorways to Going Beyond

When thinking about the Kingdom advancing and the apostolic church moving into a new dimension, I always go to the prototypes that were given us in the book of Revelation. Seventy years after the Lords' resurrection, He visited John on the Isle of Patmos where he was held in captivity for dethroning the Queen of Heaven in Ephesus. He talked to John about the seven key regional apostolic centers of that time. He explained what each had done well. He also discussed the failures that five of the seven had experienced. Then he gave a prophetic word to each one. He then admonished each one to hear what the Spirit was saying to the Church. If they would do that, they would overcome. I don't believe things have changed since then. The Lord is still telling us that we must hear what the Spirit is saying to the Church to go beyond last season's building plan and into the future. The verse that really speaks to me is Revelation 4:1. After revealing the state of that apostolic era, he then said to John: *"After these things I looked, and behold, a door standing open in heaven. And the first voice which I heard was like a trumpet speaking with me, saying, 'Come up here, and I will show you things which must take place after this.'"* In other words, he said, "John, come beyond how you presently see the Church and let Me reveal another era to you." I hear the Lord saying the same thing to us now, and I hope this book by Robert Heidler and me helps you understand the era ahead.

Though we are in a great war, for the believer in Christ, the best is always ahead. We have a wonderful promise for our future—the promise of eternal communion with God. The Bible clearly tells us that we should not live on earth with our sights set only on what is temporal; we should have a view of eternity and operate from heaven's perspective. God will give us grace to endure what is going on in our temporal world until we come into the fullness of our eternal destiny, which is with Him. This really is the bottom line. The war will intensify, but the best for God's children lies on the road ahead!

Endnotes

1 Chuck D. Pierce, *A Time to Triumph*, (Chosen Books, 2016).

2 Alain Caron, *Apostolic Expansion: The Kingdom War for Territorial Gains*, (Hodos Publishing, 2019).

3 Alain Caron, *Apostolic Centers: Shifting the Church, Transforming the World* (Arsenal Press, 2013); Chuck D. Pierce and Robert Heidler, *The Apostolic Church Arising*, (Glory of Zion International Ministries, 2015).

4 <http://pearlharbor75thanniversary.com/the-gathering-storm>, [5-13-2019].

5 Lora Allison, *The Plowman Shall Overtake the Reaper*, (Vision Publishing, 2019).

6 Tim Sheets, *The New Era of Glory: Stepping Into God's Accelerated Season of Outpouring and Breakthrough!*, (Destiny Image, 2019).

7 Venner J. Alston, *Next Level Spiritual Warfare: Advanced Strategies for Defeating the Enemy*, (Baker Publishing Group, 2019).

8 Barbara Wentroble, *The Council Room of the Lord: Accessing the Power of God*, (International Breakthrough Ministries, 2018).

Part 2

The Church Jesus Planted

by Robert Heidler

4

The Church We've Known

When I was growing up, back in the 1950s, America was much more of a "Christian nation" than it is today. Public schools started their day with prayer and Bible reading. Football games, high school graduations, and other public events also often began with prayer. Christianity was an unquestioned part of American life. Almost everybody I knew considered themselves to be Christians, and *everybody* knew what "church" was.

Church was the big building down on the corner with a tall pointy "steeple" on top. Inside the church were rows of uncomfortable bench seats called "pews." The church's windows were usually made of colorful stained glass, often depicting scenes from the Bible, and there was a big wooden box in the front called a "pulpit."

On Sunday mornings, most people went to church. (They would usually get there late, because the kids couldn't find their shoes.) Dressed in uncomfortable clothing, they would sit in the pews and sing songs from a special book called a "hymnal" while someone played slow music on an organ.

Then a man—sometimes wearing a shirt with a funny-looking collar—would walk up, stand behind the pulpit, and start to talk. He talked for a long time. As he talked, the kids would fidget in their seats and draw pictures on their church bulletins, while the adults tried very hard not to fall asleep. At some point, ushers would come and pass "collection plates" and most people would put an "offering envelope" in the plate. Then everyone went home for Sunday dinner, congratulating themselves that they have done their religious duty for the week. They have made God happy. They had gone to church!

Since the 1950s, the church has experienced many changes. Many newer churches don't have steeples and stained glass. In many cases, comfortable chairs have replaced the hard, wooden pews. Video projectors have replaced hymnals, and worship bands have replaced the organ.

Yet surprisingly, our basic concept of church has remained pretty much the same. It doesn't matter if your church is Catholic, Protestant, Pentecostal, or Charismatic.

Church is a building you go to on Sunday morning. You sing some songs, give an offering, and listen to a sermon. You do those things because you've been told that it will make God happy.

I think it would shock most Christians to learn that that whole concept of church is totally foreign to the New Testament. What we think of as "church" has almost nothing in common with the kind of churches the apostles founded.

As we see the society around us plunging into ever deeper levels of sin and depravity, many Christians have begun to cry out for a spiritual awakening. We want a move of God that will change our nation. But to experience the kind of revival we want, we must first gain a new picture of what church is supposed to be.

5

Searching for Revival

Many Christians are praying for revival. For many of us, our hearts have been stirred by reading accounts of the great revivals of the past.

Some of us remember the Jesus Movement. In the Jesus Movement, the Holy Spirit fell unexpectedly on thousands of "hippies" all over the world. At that time, Hippies were considered to be society's outcasts. Many of them were strung out on drugs, and most of them had thoroughly rejected conventional morality.

But suddenly, all over the world, thousands of hippies were getting saved. Identifying themselves with pictures of Jesus, (Who was usually portrayed with long hair and a beard), they joyfully called themselves "Jesus People."

But these long-haired Jesus People didn't look like "Christians" to many in the church. They often showed up at church wearing love beads, sandals, and bell-bottom blue jeans. They were looked at with deep suspicion.

Many churches were not happy to receive these new converts. Some churches actually stationed ushers at the door to turn them away. One speaker expressed the response of much of the church to the Jesus People as, "They don't *look* like Christians. They don't *smell* like Christians. They don't even *park* like Christians!"

But they were saved! Many of them were *thoroughly* saved. They had experienced a life-changing encounter with a supernatural God. They were passionately in love with Jesus and militantly evangelistic.

Though much of the church initially rejected the Jesus People, many eventually embraced them. The Jesus Movement infused new life into the church, particularly in the area of worship, and resulted in more than two million people being saved worldwide. Many well-known leaders in the church today have their roots in the Jesus Movement revival.

That's the kind of revival we want to see again. Too often, the churches we know seem powerless and ineffective. We are not reaching the "hard core" lost. We're barely able to reach our own children. Church is not "working." Our nation is not being reached.

We long for an invasion of the Holy Spirit. We want to experience a flow of God's power, where miracles take place, lives are changed, thousands of unbelievers are saved, and nations are transformed.

We pray for God to release a surge of anointing that will change everything. Revival has been the focus of thousands of prayer meetings.

But let me tell you a secret... **God longs for revival more than the church does!**

God *wants* to bring revival to His church!

Our problem is that we don't understand revival.

What is Revival?

Often, when churches pray for revival, what they're really asking is this: "Lord, let us keep doing the same things we've always done, the same way we've always done them… *but let them start to WORK!*"

To put it another way, when we pray for revival we're often asking God to pour some of His new wine into our old wineskin.

There have been times when God has done that. There have been incredible moves of the Spirit even though the church was an old wineskin. But the results have often been tragic.

The best example is the Welsh revival. A little over a hundred years ago, revival swept through the nation of Wales. It was one of the greatest revivals in history. The Spirit of God moved from county to county through the nation.

His presence was tangible. People walking down the street would be hit by the power of the Holy Spirit, fall to their knees in repentance and get saved.

Within a very short time, the country was transformed. Every part of society was affected. Drunkenness disappeared. Crime became almost nonexistent. Church attendance skyrocketed.

Those who study revival love to talk about the Welsh revival. But none of them want to talk about the nation of Wales today.

We might assume a revival like that would bring a permanent change… that for generations to come, people would talk about the great revival that transformed their country.

But that has not happened.

The Welsh revival was a great move of the Holy Spirit, but the Welsh church was an old wineskin. Its old structure quickly quenched the results of revival.

If you visit Wales today, a little more than 100 years after that great revival, you'll find one of the least Christian countries in Europe. Some estimate that only about 5% of the Welsh people are born-again. The New Age movement, witchcraft and Islam are growing rapidly. Most Welsh people have never *heard* of the Welsh revival. Many of those who *have* heard of it think of it as some kind of legalistic, religious movement somewhere back in their history. The old wineskin allowed the new wine to pour out and the wineskin was destroyed.

God doesn't want that to happen again. God wants to prepare a wineskin that can hold his new wine! That's why Jesus said, "New wine *must* be poured into new wineskins."

The anointing of God is the new wine, but only God's new wineskin can hold it.

True revival is not just an anointing. It's not just a sense of God's presence or a momentary flow of God's power.

True revival is the *restoration* of the life and power of the early church.

The early church had powerful anointing, but it had more than an anointing. The early church had a God-given PLAN. It was a plan that enabled it bring great transformation, and to expand with power throughout the world. Apart from that plan, revival anointing cannot be sustained.

A Revival That Lasts

Most of the revivals we read about didn't last very long. After a few months, the Presence of God departed. Things got "back to normal." Many of the greatest revivals of modern history only lasted a year or two. Those who experience a revival sometimes spend the rest of their lives looking back and telling stories of how great things were "in the revival."

I was part of the renewal movement of the 90s. While probably not a true revival, it was a wonderful visitation of the Spirit. In our region, a group of pastors gathered for prayer every week, and the Spirit always showed up. We had renewal services on Friday nights where everyone ended up on the floor under the Spirit's power. There were incredible testimonies of healing and transformation. Several times a year we hosted large conferences attended by thousands.

About three years into the movement, the leader of the renewal in our area shared a disturbing fact. Addressing the pastors in the leadership group, he said, "Most moves of the Spirit don't last longer than 5 years. That means, at most, we might have about 2 years left. We need to start thinking about how we will "wind things down" when it ends.

That was a distressing thought, but I also knew his observation was correct. Most moves of God don't last long. People pray for 20 years for revival, and when it hits, it sometimes only lasts a few months.

That didn't happen in the early church.

In the early church, they experienced *centuries* of revival. They walked in sustained, *multigenerational* revival.

How did they do it?

6

A Church in Perpetual Revival

The New Testament church lived in *continual* revival. The Presence of God came upon the church at Pentecost and *did not depart.* The early church experienced what no other brand of Christianity has ever been able to reproduce: a *perpetual* revival lasting hundreds of years. *A sustained multigenerational* revival. It spread *everywhere*, and nothing in the world could stand against it.

By the end of the first century, the early church had spread throughout the known world. It extended from India on the East to England on the West, and from Germany on the North to Ethiopia on the South. Its expansion amazed the world. In one city, when Paul and Silas came to town, the pagans cried out in horror, "These men who have *turned the world upside down* have come here also!" *(Acts 17:6 KJV).* Wouldn't you love for people to say that when *you* come to town?

It was not unusual for a church to be planted in a city and rapidly grow to 20 or 30,000 members.

Let's look at some examples of the early church's astounding growth.

The Jerusalem Church

On the day of Pentecost, the Holy Spirit fell on 120 people in the city of Jerusalem. By the end of that day, the church had grown to 3000 men and women.

Within about a year, the church more than tripled in size, numbering more than ten thousand people.[1]

Some historians estimate that by the time of Stephen's martyrdom (as early as two years later) the church in Jerusalem had grown to about 20,000 members.

In their alarm, the religious leaders in Jerusalem tried to slow the growth of the church through persecution. They were unsuccessful. Despite severe persecution at times, the church continued to grow.

Large numbers of Jews believed in Jesus. In Acts 21:20, James reports on the situation in Jerusalem with a triumphant boast, "Behold, how many *thousands* of Jews have believed!" In the Greek, that boast is even more impressive. The Greek word here is *muriades (myriad)*, which literally means *"tens of thousands."*

The Jerusalem church at that time numbered *many* tens of thousands of believing Jews! Large numbers of the Jewish priests believed (Acts 6:7). Even Pharisees believed (Acts 15:5). It is possible that, at its peak, the church made up half the population of the city of Jerusalem.

The pattern of rapid growth seen in the Jerusalem church was followed wherever the church went.

The Ephesus Church

Another example of the church's growth is seen in the church at Ephesus. Acts 19 indicates that Paul went to Ephesus, started a church, and remained there for two years teaching his converts. During those two years, not only was the entire city of Ephesus evangelized (a city of around 200,000 people), but all of the cities in the surrounding province were also reached. The church in

Colossae, as well as the seven churches mentioned in Revelation 2 and 3, were all probably planted during that two-year period.

The church in Ephesus grew so rapidly it disrupted the city's economy. Ephesus was the home of the Temple of Artemis (also known as Diana), which was one of the seven wonders of the ancient world. One of the main industries in Ephesus was the manufacture of idols depicting the goddess. But during Paul's two-year stay in Ephesus, so many people were converting to Christianity that hardly anyone wanted to buy idols. The idol makers were losing business.

One of the idol makers, a silversmith named Demetrius, called together others of his trade and complained, "This fellow Paul has convinced and led astray large numbers of people here in Ephesus and in practically the whole province of Asia. He says that man-made gods are no gods at all."

The idol makers were so angered by their loss of business, they fomented a riot. Acts 19:29 tells us, "Soon the whole city was in an uproar."

Can you imagine the church today making that kind of an impact on a city? Picture what it would be like if so many people were coming to Jesus through your church that the drug dealers and porno shop owners rioted in the streets to protest their loss of customers!

By the time Paul wrote his first letter to Timothy around A.D. 63, the church in Ephesus had probably grown to around sixty thousand members. No wonder Timothy felt intimidated when Paul installed him as the apostolic leader of that congregation. At its height, the church in Ephesus may have had as many as 100,000 members. The early Christians literally "took the city" for Jesus.

In the year A.D. 112, about eighty years after Pentecost, the Roman author Pliny wrote a letter to Emperor Trajan. In this letter, he complained that in the province of Asia Minor, where Ephesus was, "…temples to the [pagan] gods are almost totally forsaken and Christians are everywhere a multitude."[2]

The Church In Rome

Perhaps the best "case study" of the early church's amazing growth is found in the city of Rome.

In the first century, Rome was the most important city in the world. It was not only the capital of the world's greatest empire; it was the world's largest city, with a population estimated to be over a million people. (At that time, the total world population was probably about two hundred million, which means that 1 out of every 200 people on the planet lived in the city of Rome.)

The Bible doesn't tell us how the church in Rome began.

Acts 2:10 says that on the day of Pentecost, there were in Jerusalem visitors from Rome, both Jews and proselytes. It's likely that some of those Jews who got saved on Pentecost eventually returned to Rome and started a house church. Over the course of several years, that church multiplied.

We know that the early church grew with incredible speed wherever it was planted, but in most cities we can only guess at its size. In Rome, however. we have a way to measure the harvest. The city of Rome has an estimated six hundred miles of catacombs burrowed under the city. From the first century to the third, those tunnels were the city's cemeteries. Millions of people were buried in catacomb tombs during those years.

It's easy to identify which of the tombs were Christian tombs because Christians tended to decorate their tombs with Christian symbols and pictures of biblical events. By studying the catacombs, archeologists have been able

A Church in Perpetual Revival

to give us a fairly accurate picture of the church's size. They tell us that from the persecution under Nero (AD 64) until Constantine legalized Christianity in AD 313, the city's Christian population ranged in size from 175,000 to 400,000 believers. Based on this, some estimate that at the close of the first century, the church in Rome may have numbered 200,000 people, or one-fifth of the population of the city![3]

Can you envision that kind of church growth taking place in a major city today? The Roman church probably began around the middle of the first century with a single house church. That church likely numbered 20 people or less. But that little church multiplied. It went from one house church to two, and then to four, and then to eight.

Through fifty years of sometimes severe persecution, the multiplication continued, until by the end of the century the church numbered 200,000 members. Assuming that an average house church numbered about 20 people, by the end of the first century there would have been more than *ten thousand* house churches scattered across the city of Rome!

That's church growth! The pagan Romans had no way to stop the growth of the church.

Beyond Rome

As the church operated in the power of the Holy Spirit, the harvest came in. The church at Rome became an apostolic center, sending out teams to all parts of the Empire and beyond.

You've heard the saying, "All roads lead to Rome." That also means, from Rome you can go anywhere.

So teams went out from Rome and planted churches in everywhere. Justin Martyr, about the middle of the second century, writes, "There is no people, Greek or barbarian, or of any other race … whether they dwell in tents or wander about in covered wagons—among whom prayers and thanksgivings are not offered in the name of the crucified Christ."[4]

Around AD 200, Tertullian wrote to the pagan Romans in his *Apologia*, "We have filled every place belonging to you—cities, islands, castles, towns, assemblies, your very camp, your tribes, companies, palace, senate, forum. We leave you your temples only. We can count your armies; our numbers in a single province will be greater."[5]

That's called harvest.

The church historian Philip Schaff writes, "It may be fairly asserted, that about the end of the third century the name of Christ was known, revered, and persecuted in every province and every city of the empire," and, "In all probability, at the close of the third century the church numbered ten millions of souls."[6]

Some historians have speculated that by the end of the third century, *half of the population of the Roman Empire* had converted to Christianity.[7]

This growth took place within a totally pagan, occult, immoral culture, during times of severe persecution.

Endnotes

1   Acts 4:4 says the church numbered more than five thousand males. Counting adult males was a common way of numbering a community in those days. If the church numbered five thousand males, its total population was probably well over ten thousand!

2   *Pliny to Trajan*, (Epp. X.97).

3   <https://www.biblegateway.com/resources/encyclopedia-of-the-bible/Church-at-Rome> [8-5-2019] "Church at Rome." Quoting E. M. Blaiklock, Cities of the New Testament, (Fleming H. Revell, 1965), p. 86. See also, <https://www.christiancourier.com/articles/669-lessons-from-the-catacombs-of-rome> [8-1-2019] Jackson, Wayne. "Lessons from the Catacombs of Rome." quoting E. M. Blaiklock, The Archaeology of the New Testament, (Grand Rapids: Zondervan,1970).

4   Phillip Schaff, *History of the Christian Church, Chapter I: The Spread of Christianity.* § 7. Extent of Christianity in the Roman Empire <http://www.ccel.org/s/schaff/history/2_ch01.htm> [12-20-2005].

5   Phillip Schaff, *History of the Christian Church, Chapter I: The Spread of Christianity.* § 4. Hindrances and Helps. <http://www.ccel.org/s/schaff/history/2_ch01.htm> [12-20-2005].

6   Phillip Schaff, *History of the Christian Church, Chapter I: The Spread of Christianity.* § 7. Extent of Christianity in the Roman Empire <http://www.ccel.org/s/schaff/history/2_ch01.htm> [12-20-2005].

7   "Some older writers… even represent the Christians as having at least equaled if not exceeded the number of the heathen worshippers in the empire." *Phillip Schaff, History of the Christian Church, Chapter I: The Spread of Christianity.* § 7. Extent of Christianity in the Roman Empire, NOTES. <http://www.ccel.org/s/schaff/history/2_ch01.htm> [12-20-2005].

7

The Miraculous Church
The Surprising Key to the Early Church's Growth

How did the early church do it? What so attracted the pagans to Christianity that they would risk terrible persecution to align themselves with the church?

Those who have studied the early church offer an answer to that question, but it's an answer most Christians today have a hard time accepting. They tell us that a primary reason for the church's amazing growth was a common belief among the pagans that Christians had *supernatural powers.*

The noted historian Kenneth Scott Latourette says that pagans were attracted to the church "by the miracles of healing wrought in the name of Christ."[1]

Phillip Schaff tells us that pagans were drawn to the church by "the testimony of the miracles."[2]

Morton Kelsey writes, "Christian churches came to be regarded as healing shrines, competitive with the shrines of Aesculapius and other Greek gods."[3]

Schaff describes the church's reputation for miracles this way, "The Jew and the Chaldean could scarcely rival [the church's] exorcists, and the legends of continual miracles circulated among its followers."[4]

So these respected historians tell us that a rumor had spread among the pagans that Christians possessed supernatural powers to heal the sick, perform miracles, and break demonic oppression. Pagans might ridicule, or even persecute Christians at times, but when their children were seriously ill, they would often turn to the church for help.

How did the early Christians gain this reputation for being healers and miracle workers? If we accept the testimony of the New Testament, this reputation shouldn't surprise us. The New Testament consistently describes the early church as a supernatural entity, characterized by the miraculous. In both the book of Acts and the epistles, the members of the church are described as possessing "spiritual gifts" that enabled them to operate in supernatural realms. To deny the miraculous power exercised by the early Christians is to reject the clear testimony of Scripture.

But that's hard for many Christians today to grasp. Christians in America today are known for many things, but "supernatural power" is usually not on the list.

But Christians in the first few centuries were *expected* to have supernatural powers! When you became a Christian, that was part of the package, and one of the goals of the church was to equip every believer to use those powers effectively.

That was always God's plan for the church. God never intended for the church to operate apart from His power. From a New Testament perspective, a church without healing and miracles is like an elephant without a trunk, or a camel without a hump. It is still a church, but it is missing something. It is missing the very thing that is supposed to be its most distinctive feature.

As we read the New Testament, we discover that the church was *promised* miracles, it was *birthed* in miracles, and it *grew* through miracles. Miracles were an *expected* part of the lifestyle of the early Christians.

The Promise of Miracles

In John 14:12 Jesus promised, "He who believes in Me, *the works that I do shall he do also;* and *greater works* than these shall he do; because I go to the Father."

Few Christians today take this verse seriously. There is almost *no* expectation that a Christian today could do the same kinds of works Jesus did. Yet this verse is just as much a promise from God as John 3:16.

If we truly believe the Bible, we must see that Jesus is making an incredible offer. He assures us that if we have faith, we *will* experience miracles. There is no fine print. There are no exclusions. This offer did not expire in A.D. 95. The early church walked in the reality of this promise, and we can too.

A Church Birthed in Miracles

The church was born on the day of Pentecost, in Acts chapter two. The whole focus of that chapter is on a great outpouring of miraculous power: the roar of a *mighty wind* heard throughout Jerusalem, visible *flames of fire* separating and resting upon the apostles, the release of supernatural ability to speak in *unknown tongues*, and a manifestation of *God's presence* that caused the apostles to appear drunk. God was birthing the church as a *supernatural entity*, and its inception was marked by miracles.

Evangelism Through Miracles

In Rom 15:18-19 Paul wrote that he led Gentiles to salvation, "*by the power of signs and miracles, through the power of the Spirit.*" To Paul, miracles were not an optional extra in the Christian life. They were not just a curiosity. To Paul, miracles were *essential* to his evangelistic method. Miracles demonstrated the reality of his message. Paul did not want men's faith to rest on his intellectual arguments but on a *demonstration* of God's *power*. (I Cor. 2:4-5)

In the book of Acts, miracles were the primary means of drawing men and women to Jesus. It is difficult to find even one instance in Acts where someone came to Jesus apart from signs and miracles.

A Lifestyle of Miracles

I Cor. 12-14 describe miracles, healings, tongues, and prophetic words as *ordinary* occurrences in the early church. As the church gathered together, it was *expected* that some would prophesy, some would speak in tongues, and some would have an anointing to heal and perform miracles.

In Gal 3:5, Paul writes, "Does He who provides you with the Spirit *and works miracles among you*, do it by the works of the Law, or by hearing with faith?" I love the way Paul says this. Paul *takes it for granted* that miracles *are occurring* in the Galatian churches.

The *Interpreter's Bible* comments, "There can be no question that the first Christians lived in *daily expectation of miracles*."[5]

In *The Decline and Fall of the Roman Empire,* Gibbon described the life of the early church this way, "The primitive Christians perpetually trod on mystic ground... They felt that on every side they were incessantly assaulted by demons, comforted by visions, instructed by prophecy, and surprisingly delivered from danger, sickness, and from death itself, by the supplications of the church."[6]

But weren't miracles supposed to cease?

Many today have been taught a doctrine known as cessationism. Cessationism teaches that miracles were initially given to validate the gospel, but were not intended to be a continuing part of Christian experience. Most cessationists believe that miracles disappeared from the church by the end of the first century.

While those who teach cessationism often create elaborate arguments to support their view, they cannot escape the fact that there are *no Biblical passages* that teach cessationism.

The closest you can come to a passage teaching cessationism is I Cor. 13:8-10, which states that when the "perfect" comes, prophecy, tongues, and supernatural knowledge will cease. Some cessationists teach that the "perfect" here refers to the New Testament, and that when the New Testament was completed, supernatural gifts ceased to operate.

The problem with this argument is that nothing in I Corinthians 13 would suggest that the "perfect" is the New Testament. Even the dispensational theologian, Charles Ryrie, admitted that the "perfect" here is a reference to the *second coming of Jesus*. That admission is pretty much a death blow to the cessationist argument. If the "perfect" is the second coming, then I Corinthians 13 teaches that supernatural gifts *are to continue* until Jesus returns![7]

In II Tim. 3:5, Paul warns against those who are satisfied with a "form of godliness" but deny it's supernatural *power*. The word "power" is the Greek word *dunamis*—the same word translated *"miracles"* in I Corinthians 14. God is not satisfied with a church that appears to be godly. He wants a church that operates in *power*.

Not only is there a lack of Biblical evidence for cessationism, it is an idea refuted by the evidence of history. A careful study of church history reveals that miracles did not *cease* at the end of the first century, but actually continued to *increase*. Miracles continued to be a normal part of church life for *centuries.*

Irenaeus, writing 100 years after the completion of the New Testament, boasts that the church in his day "frequently" saw the dead restored to life as a result of prayer.[8]

He goes on to describe other kinds of common miracles, "Some most certainly and truly **cast out demons**… Others have the knowledge of things to come, as also **visions** and **prophetic communications**; others **heal the sick** by the imposition of hands, and restore them to health. And, moreover, as we said above, even the **dead have been raised** and continued with us many years."[9]

Augustine (early 5th century) was one of the most influential theologians in history. Early in his ministry Augustine held a cessationist view. (Many cessationists today quote Augustine to support their ideas.)

After witnessing a number of dramatic miracles in his own church, however, Augustine began to write down and carefully document the miracles he observed. Within a two-year period he compiled a list of more than 70 well-attested miracles, including healings of blindness, breast cancer, gout, paralysis, hernia, and other diseases. Augustine also recounted miracles in which farm animals were cured, demons were cast out, and the dead raised. Toward the end of his life, Augustine wrote a **retraction** of his earlier cessationist statements, and devoted much of his time to a ministry of healing.[10]

Examples of documented miracles literally fill the pages of church history. Here are just a few examples:

Justin Martyr (2nd Century), "Many of our Christians have healed and do heal, driving possessing spirits out of men, though they could not be cured by all the other exorcists, or by those who used incantations and drugs."[11]

Theophilus of Antioch (2nd Century) "Physical healing is evidence that the power of the resurrection is already working in us. Death is being put to flight."[12]

Irenaeus (2nd Century) "Those who are His disciples do in His name perform [miracles] so as to promote the welfare of other men, according to the gift which each one has received."[13]

Theodotus (late 2nd Century) confirmed that the signs of the Spirit, healings and prophecies, were still being performed by the church in his day.[14]

Origin (3rd Century), "Christians expel evil spirits and perform many cures and foresee certain events."[15]

Novatian (3rd Century), The Holy Spirit "places prophets in the church, instructs teachers, directs tongues, gives powers and healing, does wonderful works… and orders whatever other gifts there are to make the Lord's church perfected and completed."[16]

Tertullian (3rd Century) lists a wide range of diseases he has seen cured. He also describes a number of times when Roman officials who, in times of persecution, dismissed charges against Christians because a friend or relative had been healed by a Christian.[17]

In his book, *Healing and Christianity,* Kelsey writes, "The prevailing acceptance of healing as a norm in the Christian church appears from many sources. In the very early Shepherd of Hermas we find a fascinating reference to those who did NOT undertake to relieve illness and distress in the Christian way… "He therefore," Hermas wrote, "that knows the calamity of such a man, and does not free him from it, commits a great sin, and is guilty of his blood."

Kelsey concludes, "healing was part of a total framework in which Christians were educated: a reality of religious experience in which they participated… And indeed, if they were to follow the teachings of Christ, it is hard to see how they could do otherwise."[18]

Miracles Are Our Birthright.

Miracles were never intended to cease. In fact, dramatic miracles are still taking place in the church today. There are millions of Christians in the world today for whom miracles are a normal part of life.

In my first book, *Experiencing the Spirit*, I used the illustration of what God is doing in China. "The majority of China's 50 to 75 million believers have come to faith in Jesus as a result of witnessing the miraculous power of God. Deng Zhaoming, editor of the ecumenical Chinese magazine *Bridge* and a distinguished China watcher comments, 'In the church of China, at least 50 percent of believers became Christians through a remarkable healing taking place in their family.'"[19]

But miracles are not only intended for those living "long ago and far away." Miracles are intended for YOU. God wants *every* believer to live a supernatural life, bathed in the divine power of a mighty Creator God.

God wants every church to operate in the power the early church experienced.

The problem is, most of the church today has not "equipped the saints" to do it. Most Christians have never been taught how to pray for healing, or operate in supernatural power.

So we've seen two things about the early church:

1. They moved in CONTINUAL REVIVAL. Through the power of the Spirit, the church grew explosively, and nothing had the power to stop it.

2 They moved in SUPERNATURAL POWER. Christians were looked at as "miracle workers." Signs, wonders, and supernatural healing were an expected part of church life.

Neither of these things "just happened." They did not occur by accident. They were a result of the PLAN Jesus had given His church. In the rest of this book, we want to look at Jesus' plan.

Endnotes

1   Kenneth Scott Latourette, *A History of Christianity*, (Harper & Brothers, 1953), p. 107.

2   Philip Schaff, *History of the Christian Church,* Vol. 2, P 16 <classicchristianlibrary.com/library/schaff.../Schaff-History_of_Christian_Church-v2.pdf> [6-3-2019].

3   Morton T. Kelsey, *Healing and Christianity: A Classic Study*, (Augsburg Books, 1995), Kindle edition, Amazon Digital Services LLC, 1995, [Location 1612].

4   Philip Schaff, *History of the Christian Church, Vol II* Ante Nicene Christianity A.D. 100-326. Ninth Edition, (New York: Charles Soribner's Sons, 1910), p 18.

5   Geddes MacGregor, *Interpreter's Bible*, commentary on Acts 9:53, quoted by Morton T. Kelsey, Healing and Christianity: A Classic Study, (Augsburg Books, 1995), p. 123.

6   Edward Gibbon, and D. M. Low, *The Decline and Fall of the Roman Empire,* vol. 2, (New York: Harcourt, Brace, 1960), Chap 15. p. 39-40.

7   Charles Caldwell Ryrie, *The Ryrie Study Bible: New American Standard Translation* (Chicago: Moody Press, 1976), p.1744.

8   Eusebius, *Ecclesiastical History*, book V, chapter VII, (Grand Rapids: Baker Book House, 1973). p. 186.

9   Ibid. p. 187.

10   Augustine, *City of God*, book 22, chapter 8.

11   <www.newadvent.org/fathers/0127.htm> [6-4-2019].

12   Morton T. Kelsey, *Healing and Christianity: A Classic Study*, (Augsburg Books, 1995), Kindle edition, Amazon Digital Services LLC, 1995, [Location 1623].

13   <https://www.samstorms.com/enjoying-god-blog/post/spiritual-gifts-in-church-history--2- [7/22/19].

14   <https://www.samstorms.com/enjoying-god-blog/post/spiritual-gifts-in-church-history--3- [7/22/19].

15   Origin, *Against Celsus*, i.46, ANF, 4:415.

16   Novatian, *Treatise of Novatian Concerning the Trinity*, Ante-Nicene Fathers Vol 5, trans. Robert Ernest Wallis, (Peabody, MA: Hendrickson, 1999), p. 29.

17   Tertullian, To Scapula 4.

18   Morton T. Kelsey, *Healing and Christianity: A Classic Study*, (Augsburg Books, 1995), Kindle edition, Amazon Digital Services LLC, 1995, [Location 1594].

19   Alex Buchan, "Signs and Wonders in China," Charisma & Christian Life Magazine, January 1998, p. 38.

Part 3

Keys for a Supernatural Church

by Robert Heidler

8

Pastoral or Apostolic

NOTE: This section of the book contains some material from our earlier book, Apostolic Church Arising. Even if you have recently read that book, I'd encourage you to read the material here, as it is foundational for understanding God's plan.

The Church did not just happen.

The day after Pentecost Peter didn't say; "I've got an idea. *Let's start a Church!*"

No. The Church was PLANNED. In Matthew 16:18, Jesus proclaimed; "*I WILL build My Church.*"

The church was a crucial part of Jesus' plan when He came to earth. He spent 3 ½ years preparing the first group of Apostles to establish the church. He built their faith by personally demonstrating God's power to heal the sick and perform miracles, then he sent the disciples out two by two to do the same works they'd seen Him do.

In his post-resurrection appearances, Jesus built on His earlier teachings by giving specific instructions. Acts 1:1-2 tells us that Jesus was taken up into heaven, "after giving *instructions* through the Holy Spirit to the apostles he had chosen." The word "instructions" is the Greek word *entellomai*, which means "to give orders, or commands."

The NASV expresses this well when it translates this as "after he had…

given *orders* to the apostles He had chosen." Jesus was not leaving the apostles with some helpful ideas or suggestions. He was giving them orders.

Jesus had a specific PLAN, a God-given strategy, for how the church was to be established, and it was important to Him that the apostles followed the plan.

The things we see the apostles do in the early chapters of Acts reflect the marching orders Jesus had given.

As the church followed Jesus' PLAN, it flourished. The church became a supernatural organism. Members exercised the gifts of the Spirit to win the lost, heal the sick, raise the dead, drive out demons, and transform territories.

It was no accident that the members of the early church operated in supernatural power. That's what the PLAN was designed to produce. Unfortunately, during the dark ages, Jesus' plan was abandoned.

In our previous book, *Apostolic Church Arising,* I showed that most churches today follow a very different plan than the one Jesus gave.

The Pastoral Church

Most of the churches we've known have a very simple structure.

PASTOR

][

CONGREGATION

There is a pastor.

There is a congregation.

That's what I call the Pastoral Church.

In a Pastoral Church, each church has a pastor, and it's the pastor's job to minister. Any ministry that takes place is usually done by the pastor.

A pastoral church is not geared to "equip the saints" to minister. A pastor once shared with me that he had proposed starting a "ministry training class" to train members of the church for altar ministry. The head of the church board rebuked him for it. He said, "We don't want you to train the members to minister. That's what we pay *you* to do."

Most traditional churches follow this pastoral model. The pastor is THE minister. Ministry is what he is paid to do.

Some pastors actually feel threatened if members of the congregation want to minister. His job security lies in the fact that he can do what the "laymen" can't.

In a pastoral church, the members of the congregation are considered "laymen." *Layman* means "one who is without knowledge or training." Layman is not a biblical concept. God never intended a church to be full of people without knowledge or training.

But in a traditional church, that's how members are taught to view themselves. They come to church, sing some songs, listen to a sermon, and give an offering, and never imagine that there's anything more. So they drive to the church on Sunday morning, sit in nice neat rows, and go home thinking they have made God happy by going to church.

The tragedy is, the members of the congregation sitting in those nice neat rows all have spiritual gifts! The Holy Spirit has not stopped giving His gifts.

If the "laymen" in the church are baptized in the Spirit, they have—

locked within them—incredible gifts like prophecy, healing, and miracles. The problem is, in most churches they are never encouraged to discover their gifts. They are never trained to use them, and they are never given opportunities to exercise them.

The result is that the church operates at a very low level of power, and the world is not reached.

The early church followed a different model. An apostolic model. The apostolic model of the church is based on what I call "five-fold ministry."

Five-Fold Ministry

The church we see in the New Testament followed a different plan. It was the plan Jesus gave. It's a plan designed to equip every believer to minister with great effectiveness.

Instead of one "pastor" to do the work of ministry, the New Testament church operated with five distinct and essential leadership gifts. We call these the "fivefold ministry" of the church.

These gifts are listed in Ephesians 4:11[1]. When Jesus ascended into heaven, He gave His church apostles, prophets, evangelists, pastors, and teachers. Each of these gifts has a different function, but every believer needs to receive ministry from all five.

Eph 4:12 tells us that these five unique gifts have one common purpose: to equip God's people to do the work of ministry.

In our previous book, *The Apostolic Church Arising*, I describe these gifts in detail.

Evangelists get people saved. They also release the operation of miracles, signs and wonders in the church.

Pastors act as "shepherds" of God's sheep, providing comfort, care and protection.

Prophets reveal God's heart and mind to His people, providing each believer with vision and direction.

Teachers provide understanding, instruction and training, enabling God's people to grow and fulfill their call.

Apostles set the church in order so all the other gifts can operate. They also establish individual believers in their place of ministry.

The purpose of these gifts is not to perform the ministry of the church. It's to EQUIP GOD'S PEOPLE (that's *every* believer) to minister, using the gifts God has given them.

Endnotes

1   Five-fold or 4-fold gifts? Some writers have questioned the existence of five distinct gifts in Ephesians 4:11. The Message Bible, for example, lists only four gifts: apostles, prophets, evangelists, and pastor-teachers.

To defend the idea of lumping pastors and teachers together into one "pastor-teacher" gift, these writers refer to something called the Granville Sharp rule. Granville Sharp is a rule of Greek grammar learned by every first-year Greek student. Stated simply, Granville Sharp says this:

When you find the Greek construction "article – noun – 'kai' (the Greek word for 'and') – noun," both nouns are referring to the same thing. This rule is often very helpful for interpreting the Bible. For example, if find a passage that talks about Jesus as "the Lord and Savior" Granville Sharp tells us that the words Lord and Savior are both describing the same person.

Based on the Granville Sharp rule, some writers have argued that "pastors and teachers" here must refer to the same gift, a single gift of "Pastor-Teacher."

This shows that a little knowledge can be a dangerous thing! The attempt to join the gifts of pastor and teacher into one "pastor-teacher" gift ignores an important exception to the Granville Sharp rule. Any good Greek grammar book will tell you that the Granville Sharp rule only applies when both of the nouns are singular.

When the nouns are plural, there are many examples where the two nouns in this construction are definitely not referring to the same thing. For example,

In Mt 3:7 and Acts 23:7, "Pharisees and Saducees" obviously refers to two distinct groups.

In Acts 17:18 – "Stoics and Epicureans" again are two distinct groups. Perhaps most importantly, in Eph. 2:20 and 3:5, we find this same construction for "apostles and prophets," yet apostles and prophets are clearly two distinct gifts.

So to invoke the Granville Sharp rule to try to combine pastors and teachers into one "pastor-teacher" gift is totally without justification.
Jeremy M. Schopper, in his excellent paper on this subject, concludes, "The miss-application of the Granville Sharp Rule to Ephesians 4:11 has unnecessarily blurred the distinctive natures of the offices of pastor and teacher… pastor and teacher should not be counted as one office." (Those wishing a more detailed study of this can download his paper here: http://www.docstoc.com/docs/26443284/Exposition-of-Eph-411-and-the-Granville-Sharp-Rule).

9

A Picture of Five-Fold Ministry

When I teach on the five-fold ministry, I like to lead the class in a dramatic exercise to show how five-fold ministry is supposed to operate. I ask for five volunteers to play the part of the five-fold ministers. My wife, Linda, always plays the part of the evangelist.

I begin by describing the **evangelist**. I say, "The evangelist is gifted to 'birth babies' into the kingdom. There is nothing an evangelist loves more than birthing babies. When a new Christian is born, the evangelist gets very excited."

At that point, Linda takes a cute little baby-doll from behind her back and holds it up. That doll is our *Baby Christian*. Linda hugs the doll and bounces up and down with delight. She is obviously thrilled to have a new baby in the Kingdom. Then I say something like this… "The evangelist is excited to see a new baby born into the kingdom. That excitement lasts about five minutes. Then the evangelist is ready to move on and birth another baby." So Linda casually tosses *Baby Christian* over her shoulder and moves on. Everyone in the audience gasps!

We gasp, but that's often what happens in the church. The evangelist is gifted to birth babies, but it's not the evangelist's gift to nurture and establish babies in the faith.

That's why a new Christian needs to come under the care of a **pastor**. The pastor's gift is to provide nurture, comfort and protection. The evangelist needs to entrust our *Baby Christian* to someone with a pastoral gift. (In our exercise, the person playing "pastor" runs over and picks up Baby Christian, hugs him, pats him on the head, and makes sure he's okay.)

Biblically, a pastor is not someone who sits in a church office writing a Sunday sermon. A true pastor works with people and cares for them with great compassion. He (or she) is like the nurse in the delivery room who gently cradles a newborn baby, cleans it up, makes sure it is healthy and fed and protected. We need pastors. They are a vital element in the Body of Christ.

A pastor's heart is to provide comfort, care, and protection. Our problem is that, in many churches, a pastor is all you have. Christians have been saved for 30 years and the pastor is still patting them on the head, comforting them and making sure they are well fed. God has more for us than that!

That's why we need **prophets**. In our exercise, the pastor hands *Baby Christian* to the prophet. The prophet looks at the baby, points his finger at him and says, "It's good that you are comfortable and well fed, but you have a call of God on your life! You were created with a destiny! There are things God wants you to do." So the prophet gives *Baby Christian* vision for his future. That's what prophets do. Where you have prophets, people gain vision and are highly motivated to fulfill their destiny.

But if a prophet is all you have, our *Baby Christian* may still fail, because he won't understand *how* to do what he's called to do.

So the prophet hands *Baby Christian* to the **teacher**. The teacher gets out his Bible and opens it up, "Yes, *Baby Christian*, you have a call from God,

A Picture of Five-Fold Ministry

but you need to understand some things. You need to understand how to walk with God and how to operate in God's power and how to experience God's blessing." So the teacher begins to teach and train our baby.

The evangelist, pastor, prophet, and teacher each have a crucial part to play in building believers to maturity and equipping them to minister.

The **apostle** has set that whole process in order and makes sure all these gifts are functioning. The apostle also watches carefully as *Baby Christian* moves through that progression, to be sure he is growing and developing. Finally the apostle says, "I think you are ready to be launched out into ministry." (At this point in our exercise, the person playing the apostle will take *Baby Christian* and toss him out into the audience!)

But the exercise isn't over yet.

What happens when you are launched into ministry for the first time? You often crash and burn. You sometimes come away wounded.

So the person playing the pastor rushes out to retrieve *Baby Christian* and comfort him. When you crash and burn you need to have pastors to minister to you and encourage you.

Then the prophet takes *Baby Christian* aside and says, "You messed up, but you still have a call of God on your life. Don't give up!"

Next the teacher steps in and says, "You crashed and burned because there are some things you did not understand. Let me explain some things to you."

Finally, the apostle says, "It's time for you to try again" and launches him into ministry again.

Do you see how these five gifts working together will build up believers and equip them to minister? Before long, *Baby Christian* is no longer a baby.

Under the influence of the five-fold ministry, our *Baby Christian* matures and is equipped to minister with great effectiveness.

Ephesians 4:12-16 tells us when all five of those gifts are operating together, these things take place:

- The body of Christ is built up.
- We all reach unity in the faith and in the knowledge of the Son of God.
- We become mature attaining to the measure of the fullness of Christ.
- We are no longer infants tossed back and forth by the waves.
- We will in all things grow up into Him who is the head, that is Christ.

That's what happened in the book of Acts.

The New Testament church did not slap a generic "pastor" label on all its leaders and give them all the same job description.

As you read about the church in the book of Acts you discover…

Some of the leaders were called **apostles.** (Acts 14:14)

Some were called **prophets**. (Acts 11:27)

Some were called **teachers.** (Acts 13:1)

Some were called **pastors**. (Acts 20:28 calls them shepherds, a synonym of pastor.)

Some were called **evangelists.** (Acts 21:8)

All five of these gifts were functioning in the early church. Each leader knew their gift, and no one was expected to do everything. They knew they all had to work together.

The result is, the saints were equipped to minister, the church flourished, and the world was changed.

10

Apostolic Centers

God has been speaking to His church about five-fold ministry for close to fifty years, yet until recently, very few churches have made the shift.

What's been the problem?

As I've talked with pastors, many of them tell me that they love the idea of five-fold ministry, but don't know how to get it. The major issue is usually a lack of five-fold ministers. A pastor looks out at his congregation and does not see apostles, prophets, teachers and evangelists in his church. He asks, "How can my church operate in five-fold ministry if it does not have all five?"

As I pondered this question, the Lord reminded me that the churches in the New Testament were house churches. Their average size was probably twenty people. Hardly any of these house churches would have had five-fold ministers in the congregation. So how did the early church operate in five-fold ministry?

That's when the Lord began to speak to me about apostolic centers.

As you study the book of Acts you discover that every time the church penetrated a new geographical area or new ethnic group, it established what I call an apostolic center. (I describe these in detail in the book, *Apostolic Church Arising*.)

What were apostolic centers?

- ◆ They were, first and foremost, teaching and training centers. Each apostolic center was begun by an apostolic team devoting a year or more to the intensive teaching and training of disciples. The goal was to establish a strong core of believers who operated effectively in the gifts of the Spirit. This began in Jerusalem, but we see the same thing taking place in Antioch, in Ephesus, and many other places.

- ◆ They were also sending centers. From an apostolic center, ministry teams were sent out to plant new churches in a region, strengthen existing churches, and penetrate new territories with the gospel.

- ◆ Apostolic centers frequently served as gathering places for regional celebrations. In the Old Testament, God established the pattern that regional worship gatherings be held three times a year at the biblical feasts. The early church continued that practice well into the fourth century. Christians in small isolated house churches would come together at an apostolic center for celebrations as hundreds or even thousands gathered for praise and ministry.

- ◆ Through teaching, training, and the sending out apostolic ministry teams, apostolic centers acted as hubs where all the churches in the region had access to the five-fold ministry gifts.

As a result of being connected to an apostolic center, churches in the first century were never weak and isolated. They were apostolically linked. Even a small house church had access to the ministry of apostles, prophets, teachers, pastors and evangelists. The result was that the churches flourished.

Through apostolic centers, every believer could be trained and equipped to minister in the Holy Spirit's power. (Jn 14:12) The miraculous became common.

So the first part of Jesus' plan for the church was an apostolic *structure* called five-fold ministry. Instead of one overworked pastor trying to do all of the ministry by himself, you have five distinct gifts working together to equip *every believer* to minister.

The key to making that work was the apostolic center, where even very small house churches had full access to five-fold ministry.

But there was more to Jesus' plan for the church than five-fold ministry! In Acts chapter two, we see the church had been given a clear strategy to advance.

Part 4

A Strategy to Advance

by Robert Heidler

11

The Celebration
An Incubator for Faith and Vision

As we read about the supernatural power of the early church, it raises a question: "Why don't we see that level of power in the church today?"

We have the same **promises** they had.

We have the same **Holy Spirit** they had.

We have the same **gifts of the Spirit** they had.

We are **called to do the same things** they did.

The church today is called to raise up a people who operate in the power of the Holy Spirit to win the lost and transform territories. That was also the call of the early church. But somehow, the early church did it better.

The New Testament church didn't just talk about equipping the saints, they did it. In the early church, plain old average, everyday believers learned to operate in supernatural power through the exercise of spiritual gifts. Christians gained a reputation as healers.

Why don't we see that today?

What did the early church do that allowed them to raise up congregations full of healers, prophets, and miracle workers?

Not surprisingly, the answer is in the Bible.

In the rest of this book we want to look at some clear biblical teaching on how the early church functioned. We want to try to break off the blinders of tradition and religion, **and see God**'s plan for His church.

We saw in the last section that Jesus had a PLAN for His church, and He communicated that plan to His apostles. (Mt. 16:18, Acts 1:2)

That tells us that the things the apostles did in the first chapters of Acts were not made up on the fly. They weren't just a response to perceived needs. The apostles were following Jesus' plan. As you study the book of Acts, it's fairly easy to see what that plan was.

The day after Pentecost Peter didn't go out, rent a big building, put a steeple on top and set up a sign saying; *First Pentecostal Church of Jerusalem.*

That was not God's plan.

God gave the apostles a different plan.

To see God's plan for the church, we want to look in Acts chapter 2 to see what the apostles set in motion when the church was born.

Acts 2:41-47 tells us that after the Holy Spirit fell and Peter gave his sermon:

> *"Those who accepted his message were baptized, and about three thousand were added to their number that day. They devoted themselves to the apostles' teaching and to fellowship, to the breaking of bread and to prayer. Everyone was filled with awe at the many wonders and signs performed by the apostles. All the believers were together and had everything in common. They sold property and possessions to give to anyone who had need. Every day they continued to meet together in the temple courts. They broke bread in their homes and ate together with glad and sincere hearts,*

praising God and enjoying the favor of all the people. And the Lord added to their number daily those who were being saved."

I'd like to focus on verse 46. The Passion Translation renders verse 46 this way: "Daily they met together in the temple courts, and in one another's homes to celebrate communion. They shared meals together with joyful hearts..."

This verse gives us our first snapshot of life in the early church. It tells us that the church the apostles founded met in two different kinds of venues. They met in homes, and they met in the temple courts. For reasons I will explain later, I call these two venues the *synaxis*, and the *celebration*.

These two venues represented two very different kinds of meetings, but both were an essential part of Jesus' plan. Let's first look at the celebration.

Celebrations in the Temple Courts

It may surprise some to learn that the early Christians worshipped in the Jewish temple. But it's not surprising if you remember who the early Christians were.

The first Christians were all Messianic Jews. They were, in fact, more "Jewish" than any Messianic Jews today. Although they were sometimes perceived as a threat by the religious establishment, these Messianic Christians were popular with the common people and were accepted as a legitimate part of Judaism.

As Jews, they were free to use the temple facilities, which offered several large open-air courts and a large covered area called Solomon's Porch.

So the early Jerusalem church worshipped every day in the courtyards

A TRIUMPHANT KINGDOM

of the temple. The purpose of these celebrations was to provide an incubator for faith and vision.

Notice some things about these gatherings:

These were *large* gatherings. (Remember, the church began with 3,000 people and multiplied from there.)

These were joyful *celebrations*. These gatherings were not times of dry, academic, teaching.

To picture what these gatherings might have been like, I think it's helpful to understand the kind of celebrations these Jewish believers were accustomed to having in the temple. These 3000 new believers had been raised as observant Jews. They had attended praise gatherings in the temple since they were little children. When they came into the temple courts, they had a clear expectation of what they might experience, and how they could participate.

Some today assume that worship in the Jewish temple would have been sedate and quiet, with priests in long robes singing songs that sounded like a funeral dirge.

That's not how it was!

Jewish worship was emotional. The ancient Jews believed in expressing their excitement and love for God openly. When celebrations were held in the temple, there were usually lots of instruments, processions and dancing, loud shouting and celebration. Sometimes, temple celebrations could get pretty wild.

Remember the accounts of David dancing as the ark was brought in to Jerusalem? We're told he "worshipped the Lord with all his might."

Think about the worship described in Psalm 150, where we are exhorted to praise the Lord loudly with every kind of instrument, along with singing and dancing!

That's a picture of worship at the Jewish Temple. I love the accounts of the all-night praise gatherings that took place in the temple courts during the Feast of Tabernacles.

The Jewish Talmud describes the festivities in detail. First, an immense candelabrum was set up in the Temple courtyard, generating such intense light that it illuminated every courtyard in the city. While Levites played flutes, trumpets, harps, and cymbals, there were torchlight processions, with men "dancing ecstatically to the hand-clapping, foot-stomping, and hymn-singing crowds."

A highlight of these night-time gatherings involved Jewish priests juggling flaming torches. One priest, Rabbi Simon ben Gamaliel, was famous for the fact that he could juggle eight flaming torches at the same time![1] (Some Christians complain about the use of flags and banners in worship. What would they say if the worship leader started juggling flaming torches?)

While I seriously doubt that Peter and John juggled any torches, I think the early church's corporate celebrations would have easily rivaled the Feast of Tabernacles celebration for sheer excitement.

After all, these meetings were led by apostles who had just seen Jesus raised from the dead and ascend into Heaven! Not only that, they had just been baptized in the Holy Spirit!

And then there were the 3,000. These were 3,000 brand-new Christians! (Remember how you felt when you first got saved?)

Not only that, they had also just been baptized in the Holy Spirit!

It would have been a time of heady excitement. The Apostles were performing signs, wonders, and miracles! More and more Jews were receiving

Jesus' message! There was a constant influx of new believers.

These early Christians were living in the miraculous. Jesus had been raised from the dead, releasing resurrection power to his church, and the result was great signs and wonders.

Acts 3 describes one impromptu gathering in the temple courts this way:

> *One afternoon Peter and John went to the temple for three o'clock prayer. As they came to the entrance called the Beautiful Gate, they were captured by the sight of a man crippled from birth… When he noticed Peter and John going into the temple, he begged them for money…*
>
> *Peter said, "I don't have money, but I'll give you this—by the power of the name of Jesus Christ of Nazareth, stand up and walk."*
>
> *Peter held out his right hand to the crippled man. As he pulled the man to his feet, suddenly power surged into his crippled feet and ankles. The man jumped up, stood there for a moment stunned, and then began to walk around. As he went into the temple courts with Peter and John, he leapt for joy and shouted praises to God.*
>
> *When all the people saw him jumping up and down and heard him glorifying God, they realized it was the crippled beggar they had passed by in front of the Beautiful Gate. Astonishment swept over the crowd, for they were amazed over what had happened to him.*
>
> *Dumbfounded over what they were witnessing, the crowd ran over to Peter and John, who were standing under the covered walk-*

way called Solomon's Porch. (Acts 3:1-11 Passion Bible).

Surrounded by a crowd that probably numbered in the thousands, Peter preached a fervent evangelistic message, and many responded. We're told that this event added at least 2000 more people to the church's swelling numbers. The result was, "All the people praised God, thrilled over the miraculous healing of the crippled man." (Acts 3:21 Passion Bible).

Amazingly, this was not a "one time" event. Notice what Acts 5 says…

The apostles performed many signs, wonders, and miracles among the people. And the believers were wonderfully united as they met regularly in the temple courts in the area known as Solomon's Porch. No one dared harm them, for everyone held them in high regard.

Continually more and more people believed in the Lord and were added to their number—great crowds of both men and women… Great numbers of people swarmed into Jerusalem from the nearby villages. They brought with them the sick and those troubled by demons—and everyone was healed. (Acts 5:12-17 Passion Bible)

No wonder the church grew! They were so excited about Jesus they started to meet like this every day.

Imagine what attending daily celebrations like that would do for your faith. Miracles were not only taught, they were openly demonstrated on a regular basis.

Contrast that with what most believers today experience. In most churches today, healing and miracles are not part of the program. They are not performed. They are not expected. They are not encouraged. In many churches, members are taught that God is not interested in healing anymore. Christians are actually *taught* unbelief!

But when the Early Church met in their large celebrations, there was not only enthusiastic praise and apostolic preaching, but also signs and wonders and miracles. And lots of people were getting saved.

These large corporate gatherings were important because they built the believers' faith in the reality and power of God's Spirit. When you come together in that kind of context, your faith blossoms.

The Need for Celebration

During the Dark Ages; the church lost the concept of joyful celebration. Church became solemn and mournful, a fearful place to be. Believers were no longer taught to expect the miraculous.

But the good news is; God has restored the joy! When we come together at Glory of Zion on Sunday morning, whether you're with us in person or on the webcast, there's rejoicing, there's praise, there's signs and wonders. We're doing what the early church did in the temple courts.

Celebrations Multiply

As the church spread out from Jerusalem to the hundreds of towns and villages throughout the region, believers continued to return to Jerusalem for celebrations, especially at the time of the feasts.

When the church moved into the Gentile world, however, it became less and less realistic for them to return to Jerusalem. That's one reason apostolic centers were established. For the rapidly expanding gentile church, apostolic centers took the place of Jerusalem, as central hubs for teaching, gathering, and celebration.

Ephesus was an apostolic center for churches in the Roman province of Asia. Paul reminds the Ephesians that he met with them, not only in their house churches, but also in their larger public gatherings. (Acts 20:20)

In Ephesus larger gatherings initially took place in a rented facility, the school of Tyranus, and may have spread to other venues. It was common for the early church in many places to even meet out in the open countryside.

This continued to be a pattern. Bob Fitts, Sr. wrote, "The early Church not only met in small groups in homes, but also in larger gatherings in public places."[2]

Wolfgang Simson also describes the early church operating on these two levels. He tells us that Christian neighbors would meet together in house-churches where they share their lives, but that Christians also came together for large citywide or regional celebrations.[3]

Endnotes

1 Excerpted from *Celebrate, the Complete Jewish Holiday Handbook*, © 1994 by Jason Aronson Inc. <https://www.myjewishlearning.com/article/simchat-beit-hashoavah-the-water-drawing-festival/> [7-15-2019].

2 <https://world-map.com/the-house-church-in-the-new-testament/2/s> [7-20-2019].

3 <https://www.therealchurch.com/articles/houses_that_changed_the_world.html> [7-20-2019].

12

The Synaxis
An Incubator for Spiritual Gifts

We've seen that the church came together in large celebrations that served as incubators for faith and vision.

But the early church also had another kind of meeting. They also met from house to house. (Acts 2:46) The phrase "from house to house" can also be translated: "In various private homes."[1]

That huge congregation of people who met for joyful celebrations in the temple also came together in smaller groups that met in homes.

Why did they meet in homes? Many have assumed the early church was forced to meet in homes because of persecution. That is not accurate. The New Testament shows us that the early church chose to meet in homes even when they had the freedom to also meet openly. (Acts 2:46, Acts 5:42, Acts 20:20)

Meeting in homes was not required by a need for secrecy. They chose to meet in homes because there were things that could take place in a home setting that could never happen in a large celebration.

We see house churches mentioned all through the New Testament:

- House churches in Jerusalem (Acts 2:42-47, Acts 5:42).

A TRIUMPHANT KINGDOM

- The house of Mary, mother of John Mark (Acts 12:12)
- Lydia's House (Acts 16:40)
- Titius Justus' house (Acts 18:7)
- Church in an upper room of a house in Troas (Acts 20:8)
- House churches in Ephesus (Acts 20:20)
- Priscilla and Aquila's house (Romans 16:3-5, 1 Corinthians 16:19)
- Nympha's house in Laodicea (Colossians 4:15)
- Archippa's house in Colossae (Philemon 2)
- The home of Aristobulus in Rome (Rom. 16:10)

One of the Early Church's names for these "house church" gatherings was *Synaxis*. Synaxis is a Greek word that meant "a *gathering*, a *coming together* or a *reunion*." A synaxis was a "family reunion" of their spiritual family.

In this book, I will use the term *synaxis* instead of the more common term "house church," because the idea of a house church can communicate a lot of different things to different people.

For many, "house church" may simply be an attempt to reproduce the activities of a traditional "church service" in living room. There are songs sung, a teaching given, and sometimes an offering taken. While the living room setting lends itself to more personal interaction, it is still modeled after a traditional church service.

In some places, "house church" does not even imply a smaller group. I visited a house church in China once that met in an old warehouse. There were several hundred people present, and the meeting was almost indistinguishable from what we would think of as a traditional church service.

Sometimes house churches are confused with cell groups, which can be highly structured gatherings, operating as a ministry of a larger church. Often the church leadership mandates a specific Bible study curriculum for all the cells to follow.

There's nothing wrong with any of these kinds of house churches, and all provide a great opportunity for fellowship and body life. But that's not what a first century synaxis was.

A synaxis was a very specific kind of meeting, with a very specific purpose. While synaxis gatherings are mentioned all through the New Testament, the book of I Corinthians gives us the clearest picture of what took place in these meetings.

I Corinthians reveals that synaxis meetings were designed to accomplish at least three specific things.

1. Praise and Worship. Praise and worship was an important part of a synaxis. In fact, it's part of the definition. Webster defines a synaxis as "an assembly met for worship. Especially: a congregation in the early Church."[2]

Praise and worship was an important part of the synaxis meeting, because it brought a manifestation of the presence of God. I Cor 5:4 tells us that when the church "came together" (that's the phrase the word *synaxis* comes from), a manifestation of God's presence and power was expected.

Empowerment is one of the primary goals of a synaxis. Within the context of a synaxis, believers learn to recognize God's presence and be filled with His power.

2. The Lord's Supper. The Lord's Supper was also an important ingredient of a first century synaxis. Dictionary.com defines a synaxis as, "an assembly for religious worship, especially for the celebration of the Eucharist" (the Lord's Supper).³

That's what Acts 2:46 is describing. "They met together… in one another's homes to celebrate communion. They shared meals together with joyful hearts."

Acts 2:46 links celebrating the Lord's Supper with sharing a meal. In the early church, the Lord's Supper was observed in the context of a special meal, called a love feast. These love feasts are described in I Corinthians, and also mentioned in Jude, and Peter.

In the ancient world, sharing a meal in someone's home was a sign of covenant. As the believers met together for a meal, they were saying, "We are not just committed to the Lord, we're committed to each other." Eating together signified that they were spiritual family.

I Cor 10, Paul says that when they meet, it was important that they "discern the body." Roman Catholics teach that this verse is talking about "transubstantiation," a belief that the elements of communion somehow transform into the actual body and blood of Jesus. But that's not what Paul is saying.

Paul is saying that they need to discern that the *church*—the group gathered in their living room—is the *body* of Christ! As members of Christ's body, they are a covenant community, committed to each other and members of each other. In I Cor. 10:17, he emphasizes this when he says that when we break bread together, we become one, because, "We who are many are one loaf."

This covenant commitment to each other was evidenced by the early Jerusalem church's willingness to give to members who were in need. (Remember that Jews from all over the known world were in Jerusalem when the Spirit fell. Most of them had only come prepared to stay for a week or two, but many of them chose to extend their stay in Jerusalem, to be part of the "new thing" God was forming, *the church*.)

Unfortunately, that meant many off them quickly began to run out of resources. Faced with this unprecedented need, the members of the church expressed their covenant commitment by selling possessions and giving to those in need. (Acts 2:44-45)

3. Equipping believers to exercise their spiritual gifts. One of the most important purposes of a synaxis was to be a place where believers were free to exercise spiritual gifts. The longest passage of the book of I Corinthians, chapters 12-14, gives detailed instructions for the exercise of spiritual gifts in the synaxis.

I Corinthians 12:7-11 says; "*when you come together* each one is given a manifestation of the Spirit. To one is given a word of wisdom, to another a word of knowledge, to another faith, to another gifts of healing, to another miracles, to another prophecy, to another distinguishing of spirits, to another tongues, to another interpretation.

Again, the phrase "when you come together" is the phrase the word *synaxis* comes from. A synaxis is a "coming together." I Cor. 12 tells us that when the *synaxis* gathered, the Holy Spirit distributed His gifts. According to this passage, a typical synaxis gathering would have included healings, miracles, tongues and interpretation, and prophetic words. These were normal activities in the life of the early church.

In the synaxis, every believer was encouraged to minister to those around them, exercising the gifts Holy Spirit provided. We're told, "When you come together, *everyone* has a hymn, or a word of instruction, or a prophetic word, or a tongue, or an interpretation." (I Corinthians 14:26)

Everyone was encouraged to participate, but it was not a "free-for-all." There was clear leadership, and Paul gives instructions on how to keep things moving in an orderly way.

So, as the large CELEBRATION gatherings were incubators for *faith* and *vision*, the small SYNAXIS gatherings were incubators for *gifts*.

In a synaxis, believers were given opportunity to discover, develop, and practice their gifts. It is in the context of a synaxis that the goal of Ephesians 4 was fulfilled. God's people were equipped for the work of ministry.

I believe that was a major key to the success of the early church.

Even if all of the five-fold ministers were in place, if there was not a place where believers could actually exercise their gifts, no "equipping" could occur.

But when believers are built up in faith through the celebrations, and then given opportunity to practice their gifts in the synaxis, a revival dynamic is created. The church is no longer a passive congregation. It is an army, operating in the supernatural power of God to change the world.

The Synaxis Chronicles

In the church today, we often picture the power to transform a territory coming through large crowds meeting in stadiums. Yet the real power of the early church took place in the synaxis.

How can a small synaxis create a revival dynamic that transforms a territory?

The Synaxis

To give a picture of this, I wrote a trilogy of fiction books. It's called the SYNAXIS CHRONICLES (written under the pen name, Robert David MacNeil.) In the first book of the trilogy, *IONA PORTAL*, a group of ordinary people are brought together in a synaxis, and begin to learn to use their gifts. In the process, they face demonic opposition, but succeed in opening a portal into the heavens to secure angelic help.

In the second book, *IONA STRONGHOLD*, their gifts are growing stronger, and the synaxis groups begin to multiply. The result is that a major plot of the enemy is thwarted.

In the final book, *IONA RISING*, we see synaxis groups spreading all over the world, with the result that demonic powers are defeated and territories are transformed. That's a very good picture of what actually happened in the early church!

While the books are written as fiction, many have found them helpful in gaining a vision of how the church is designed to function. The power of the church is not measured by how many people can be packed into a stadium, but by how many believers are equipped to function in the power of the Holy Spirit. (These books are available in paperback from Glory of Zion.org, and in both paperback and ebook versions at Amazon.com.)

What would a New Testament synaxis meeting have looked like? In our earlier books, *Messianic Church Arising* and *Apostolic Church Arising*, I paint a picture of a visit to a first century synaxis. For those who haven't read those books, I'd like to share a version of that description.

Endnotes

1	<https://world-map.com/the-house-church-in-the-new-testament/2/> [7-22-2019].

2	<https://www.merriam-webster.com/dictionary/synaxis> [7-22-2019].

3	<https://www.dictionary.com/browse/synaxis> [7-22-2019].

13

A Visit to a First Century Synaxis

We've seen the power of the church, how it grew and "took over" the world in the short span of 70 years. We've sensed the anointing that was upon it. But what was the early church like? What gave it such life and power?

In this chapter, I would like to take you with me to visit a synaxis in the early church. Everything I describe will be based on historical descriptions of the first century church, either in the New Testament or in other early Christian literature.

Let's imagine we are walking down a street in the city of Rome. It is A.D. 95… more than 60 years have passed since the day of Pentecost. We are about to "drop in" on a typical "house church" in that city.

The time is Saturday evening. By Jewish reckoning, the first day of the week began at sundown on Saturday. The synaxis meets in the evening because many of the people have to work during the day. We arrive at the door of a typical Roman house and are warmly welcomed by the host.

As we walk through the door, you look across the entrance into the large open courtyard of the home. There appears to be some kind of party going on. Some of the people are playing flutes, lyres, and tambourines, while others are singing, dancing, and clapping their hands.

You immediately look around to make sure you came into the right house. As you listen to the words, however, you realize that this is the right place, for the words of the songs are words of praise to Jesus. These people are overflowing with joy because they have come to know the living God.

What you are witnessing is the way the early church praised God. This type of worship is foreign to much of the church today, but from the biblical and historical records, this is what the worship in the early church was like. It was a free and joyful celebration, with a great deal of singing and dancing.

Many times the gathering would begin with the people getting in a ring (or several concentric rings) and dancing Jewish-style ring dances (like the *Hora*).

Here's how one early Christian writer described their worship:

Clement of Alexandria (writing in the third century), describes the "daughters of God" leading the church in a ring dance: "The righteous are the dancers; the music is a song of the King of the universe. The maidens strike the lyre, the angels praise, the prophets speak; the sound of music issues forth, they run and pursue the jubilant band; those that are called make haste, eagerly desiring to receive the Father."[1]

This picture of the church rejoicing before the Lord in dance comes as a surprise to many people. Many have thought of the early church's worship as somber, quiet, and almost mournful. That concept of church worship, however, did not become prevalent in the church until after the fourth century when the church was overrun by the asceticism of pagan philosophy.

So, here we are in a large courtyard. There is a great deal of singing, dancing, and rejoicing in the Lord. As the songs slow down a little, many people get down on their knees before the Lord. Most are lifting up hands to Him. A tremendous sense of the Lord's presence fills the courtyard.

A Visit to a First Century Synaxis

As we enter into the worship, we are overwhelmed by the love and acceptance of the people.

After much singing and dancing, food is brought out. People find their seats and prepare for the meal. This shared weekly meal is called the "love feast," or *Agape*.

To begin the meal, the woman of the house lights the candles, saying a special prayer of thanksgiving. Then one of the leaders stands with a cup, blesses the Lord, and passes it around so each one can drink from it. He then picks up a loaf of bread and offers thanks. It also is passed from person to person. This is the Lord's Supper in its original context.

During the meal, the members of the synaxis talk about the events of their week. They also share testimonies of what they've seen the Lord do. It's a time of intimacy and relationship-building. It feels like a family.

After the meal ends, worship continues until, at some point, a change begins to take place. There is a subtle shift in the atmosphere. The air seems to thicken. A tangible sense of the Presence of God comes and rests in the place. First Corinthians chapter five describes it this way: "When you are assembled in the name of the Lord Jesus… and the *power* of our Lord Jesus is present…"

Those who have studied revival literature recall that a *tangible sense of God's Presence* has frequently accompanied the great revivals of history. The manifest Presence of God is, in fact, the *hallmark* of true revival. In the *presence* of a holy God, sinners find salvation, backsliders find repentance, and the miraculous becomes commonplace.

In the early church, this was a weekly occurrence. When the members of the body assembled, they came as "living stones" forming the temple of God. As the presence of the Lord had once filled Moses' tabernacle (Ex. 40:34) and the temple of Solomon (II Chr. 7:1-2), so the Presence of God filled His *new* temple, the church. This is what Jesus promised, "Where two or three come together in my name, there am I with them" (Mt. 18:20).

As those assembled sense the Presence of God, some fall to the ground in worship. Others stop and are silent, welcoming the Lord's Presence.

As the Presence of God rests in their midst, ministry begins to take place. I Cor. 12 describes the Holy Spirit sovereignly manifesting His gifts as His people assemble. A woman on the far side of the courtyard gives a word of knowledge for healing. A man raises his hand and people cluster around to pray for him. He is instantly healed.

Someone else reads a passage of Scripture. Another man, a teacher, gives an explanation of the passage. A woman sings a beautiful prophetic song. Many are so touched by its beauty and anointing they begin to weep.

Prophetic words are given. There are tongues and interpretation. Through it all, they continue to move in and out of worship, singing more songs of praise. This scenario is clearly described in I Corinthians 14:23-32.

This was "ministry" in a first century synaxis. At one point a man introduces a family who have been sitting quietly near the back of the crowd. You can tell by the look on their faces that this is their first time here, and they are not sure they are in the right place. They look uncomfortable.

The man introducing them says they have come tonight because their 12-year-old daughter has contracted an illness that has left her totally blind. They've come for the church to pray for her. Those with the gift of healing come and stand with the elders as they anoint the little girl with oil and pray. Suddenly the little girl begins to cry. With tears running down her cheeks, she cries out, "I can see! I can see!"

A Visit to a First Century Synaxis

The mother crouches down and hugs her daughter. Within four or five minutes the entire family is saved, giving their hearts to Jesus.

A prophetic word is given revealing the secrets of someone's heart. That person comes forward and says, "I don't know Jesus, but I know God is here! I want to know Him!"

This is how much of the evangelism in the church took place… through the miraculous power of God working in the midst of His people. Many Christians today don't even have a concept of that happening, but it was the norm in the early church.

Irenaeus (writing around A.D. 195) tells us that in his day, prophetic words, tongues, and miracles of healing were common in the church.[2]

Our meeting of the church has now run late into the night, but no one seems to notice. Finally the meeting begins to break up. The sense of the Spirit's presence begins to lift, but there are still several small groups gathered in prayer.

As people prepare to leave, there is a great deal of hugging and kissing. It seems like a family reunion, and it is. It is the weekly reunion of the family of God.

How would you like to be part of a meeting like that? That's what the early church was. It was a temple where the glory of God dwelt. It was also a training ground, a place where every believer could be equipped to skillfully use the gifts of the Holy Spirit. On any given Saturday evening there would have been thousands of synaxis meetings like this all over the city of Rome.

That's also the kind of church they had at Antioch, Corinth, Ephesus, Colossae, and Jerusalem. That's the kind of church that took the known world in one generation.

An apostle like Paul would go into a city, start a synaxis… and the Presence of God would come. Believers were equipped and built up in their gifts. Within a few years *tens of thousands* would be saved and the entire region affected. By the end of the first Century the church had spread *everywhere,* because the pagans didn't have anything that could stand against the power of God and His supernatural church.

Incredibly, that's how the church met for over 300 years.

Endnotes

1   Clement of Alexandria, *Exhortation to the Heathen*, Chapter XII, Christian Classics Ethereal Library, <http://www.ccel.org/ccel/schaff/anf02.vi.ii.xii.html> [4-3-2006].

2   Eusebius, *Ecclesiastical History*, book V, chapter VII, (Grand Rapids: Baker Book House, 1973), p. 186-187.

Part 5

Raising Up a Supernatural Church

by Robert Heidler

14

Taking Up Your Power Tools

To understand why the synaxis was important, we need to understand some things about spiritual gifts, and what it takes to establish a supernatural church.

In I Corinthians 12, the first thing God tells us about spiritual gifts is that He does not want us to be ignorant of them.

Unfortunately, most Christians today *are*.

There has been so much confusion and contention and misunderstanding about the gifts that many churches reject them altogether.

In my book, *Experiencing the Spirit*, I begin the chapter on spiritual gifts with this story…

> *John wanted a bookshelf unit in his living room. He had seen pictures in the home magazines of floor-to-ceiling shelf units that not only held books, but were beautiful pieces of furniture. He wanted a shelf unit like the ones in those pictures. Unfortunately, he couldn't afford to buy one of these expensive units, so he decided to build his own.*
>
> *His problem was he didn't have any tools. His father had offered to give him a very nice table saw, but power tools always*

made him nervous. He'd heard stories about people accidentally cutting off their fingers with a table saw. He didn't like the noise and the sawdust they made either. Power tools seemed dangerous and messy, and he didn't want anything to do with such equipment. It even made him uncomfortable to be around other people who were using power saws.

So John decided to build a shelf unit without tools. He first bought some boards. They weren't really the length he needed, but he felt he could "make do" with shorter shelves than he had wanted.

Then he bought some bricks. He made two stacks of bricks, about a foot high, and laid a board across the top. Then he made more stacks of bricks on top of that and laid another board across. He kept adding layers until he had a shelf unit about four feet high. By the time it reached a height of four feet, the unit was so wobbly he was afraid to make it any higher for fear it would fall over.

John put his books on the shelves and stood back to admire his work. It wasn't really a beautiful piece of furniture. It looked more like an ungainly stack of bricks and boards. It was a lot smaller than he wanted it to be, and didn't hold all of his books. It wasn't very stable either. He was afraid to put too much weight on the top shelf for fear it would all fall over.

But he was still pretty proud of himself. He had a shelf unit, and he didn't have to use any tools to build it.[1]

That's the story of much of the church today. We look at the church in the New Testament, and we want to have one like it. But the tools the Father has provided for building that kind of church seem messy and frightening, and we're not quite sure how to use them, so we try to build a church without them.

The "power tools" God has provided are called spiritual gifts. They are abilities given by the Spirit, designed to equip us to build up the church. The New Testament describes these gifts as vitally important for the church. Paul's comment concerning the operation of the gifts is, "ALL of these things MUST be done" (I Cor. 14:26) for the church to be built up.

But spiritual gifts can seem messy, particularly when people are just learning to use them. On occasion they can also be dangerous. Power is always dangerous if we don't use it carefully. People can get hurt when there's power.

But without spiritual gifts, the church we build can never achieve the power and effectiveness of the New Testament church.

Spiritual gifts are important because they are the *key* to a supernatural church.

Gifts are given to *equip* God's people to do the works of Jesus. In Eph 4, we're told that the goal of the church's five-fold ministry is to "equip the saints" to do the work of ministry. But accomplishing that ministry requires the gifts of the Spirit.

So the primary goal of the five-fold ministers is to train God's people to effectively use their spiritual gifts.

But very few churches are doing that.

Many churches actually teach *against* spiritual gifts. They tell their members that the gifts are "not for today."

Other churches believe spiritual gifts are valid, but choose not to stress

A TRIUMPHANT KINGDOM

them as important. They basically choose to ignore spiritual gifts.

Some churches acknowledge the reality of the gifts, yet actually seem afraid of what might happen if the gifts were to begin to function openly. Some of them prohibit the *exercise* of gifts like tongues and prophecy in the church service. (Even though the Bible specifically tells us *not* to forbid these gifts. I Thess 5:20, I Cor 14:39)

But even churches that believe the gifts are important often don't effectively equip the saints to use them. They may do a teaching about gifts from time to time, but most of the members remain in ignorance of their gifts. The average person in the church doesn't know what their gifts are, or how they are supposed to use them.

The problem is often that many church leaders really aren't sure *how* to equip the saints to use their gifts!

The result is, the church continues to try to build itself up without the benefit of the "power tools" the Father has given.

Yet the New Testament gives a clear pattern for establishing an environment where the gifts can flourish.

Endnotes

1   Robert Heidler, *Experiencing the Spirit*, (Ventura: Regal books from Gospel Light, 1998), p. 112-113.

15

Six Things You Need to Know About Spiritual Gifts

In the last few chapters we saw that the early church met in large celebrations, but also in smaller synaxis gatherings.

To understand WHY the early church met this way, let's review a few things about spiritual gifts.

1. Spiritual gifts are supernatural abilities given by God to equip His people.

The church is the "body of Christ" on the earth today. As such, Jesus has called His church to do the same things now that He did when he was here in His physical body.

When Jesus was here in His physical body, He healed the sick. He won the lost. He prophesied. He taught. He cast out demons and performed miracles. He wants His church to follow His example.

Can Christians today really do all of those things?

Yes! In fact, Jesus promises us that we can. "Truly I tell you, whoever believes in Me will do the works I have been doing, and they will do even greater things than these, because I am going to the Father." (John 14:12 NIV)

But how can we, as ordinary human beings, do the supernatural things

Jesus did?

The answer of the New Testament is "spiritual gifts." I Cor. 12 lists nine of these spiritual manifestations. They are:

1. Word of Wisdom. – A supernatural insight to solve a problem.

2. Word of Knowledge – A piece of information supernaturally revealed.

3. Faith – A supernatural ability to know God's will and walk in faith to see it accomplished.

4. Healings – A supernatural impartation of health and well-being.

5. Miracles (The Greek word is *Dunamis*) – A supernatural ability to do the impossible.

6. Prophecy – A supernatural ability to know God's mind and heart in a situation.

7. Distinguishing of Spirits – A supernatural ability to discern the spiritual forces that are influencing events in the natural realm.

8. Tongues – A supernatural ability to speak in an unlearned language.

9. Interpretation of Tongues – The supernatural ability to interpret a tongues message.

(A more detailed explanation of these gifts may be found in Appendix 2)

In skimming through this list of gifts, one word that is found repeatedly is the word *supernatural*. A spiritual gift, by definition, is "a supernatural ability given by God to equip His people to accomplish their call."

The key word there is *supernatural*.

A spiritual gift gives an ordinary Christian the power to do things normal human beings cannot do.

I sometimes describe it this way: Being a Spirit-filled Christian is sort of like being *Superman*. Most of the time you're Clark Kent, a mild mannered Christian who sometimes raises his hands in church.

But when your spiritual gifts activate, you're like Superman. You may not be able to "bend steel in your bare hands" or "leap tall buildings in a single bound," but you are able to do things ordinary people can't do. You can do *supernatural* things.

- ◆ You can heal the sick
- ◆ You can rescue people from demonic oppression
- ◆ You can perform miracles
- ◆ You can speak a prophetic word that gives someone fresh vision and encouragement.

Learning to operate in your spiritual gift is one of the most exciting things anyone can do.

The first time you pray for someone and see them instantly healed, it does something inside you. It's the most exhilarating thing you've ever experienced. You start looking around to find someone else to pray for!

2. Spiritual gifts are the key to a supernatural church

The purpose of spiritual gifts is to enable the church to fulfill its commission. The strength and effectiveness of the church depends on the functioning of the gifts of its members. This is stressed repeatedly….

- 1 Corinthians 12:7 tells us that the manifestations (or gifts) of the Spirit are given for the "common good" (the health and strength of the church.)

- I Cor 14:1-12 stresses that the purpose of the gifts is to strengthen (or build up) the whole church.

- In I Cor 14:26, after describing the functioning of the gifts within the synaxis, Paul instructs, "all of these must be done so that the church may be built up."

That was the key to the power of the early church!

Edward Gibbon, in his classic work, *The Decline and Fall of the Roman Empire,* attributes the early church's incredible success to the "supernatural gifts" which were "ascribed to the Christians above the rest of mankind."[1]

That's why Paul insists, "All of these MUST BE DONE." The church cannot be a supernatural church without the operation of supernatural gifts.

Eph 4:12 tells us that the goal of the church's fivefold ministry is "to equip the saints to minister." That means, equipping them to use their spiritual gifts!

3. Every believer begins with at least one spiritual gift.

I Cor 12:7 tells us, "*Each believer* has received a gift that manifests the Spirit's power and presence." (Voice Bible) God wants you to know that you have at least one of those nine gifts listed in I Cor. 12.

If we really believe that, that changes our view of "church as usual."

Look around you in a typical church service, and remind yourself that everyone there possesses a supernatural gift. Some of the people sitting around you are gifted by God to heal the sick. Some of them have the gift of miracles. Some can prophesy. The problem is, most of them have never discovered their gift. They've never been taught how to use that gift. They've never been given an opportunity to exercise that gift.

So they come to church, sing some songs, listen to a sermon, and go home. And we wonder why the church seems so powerless.

But those powerful manifestations of the Spirit are still there, just waiting to be tapped.

In Romans 8:11, Paul reminds us that "the Spirit of Him who raised Jesus from the dead is living *in you*." That means, if you are a Spirit-filled Christian, the **supernatural** power that enabled Jesus' resurrection is in you *right now*.

But tragically, it's possible to have that power inside you, and never know it.

This was a real danger, even in New Testament times. In Eph 1:18 Paul tells the Ephesian Christians that he prays for "the eyes of your heart may be enlightened that you may know… His incomparably great power for us who believe." He goes on to say, "That power is the same as the mighty strength God exerted when He raised Christ from the dead."

Paul prayed for our eyes to be enlightened. He wants our eyes to be opened to see what many of us have not seen. We have the potential to operate in great power, but can still fail to understand what God has given us.

God wants you to know that the Holy Spirit possesses ALL the omnipotent power of God, and He is living in YOU. The baptism of the Holy Spirit releases the power of the Holy Spirit to flow through you. (If you've never experienced the baptism of the Holy Spirit, Appendix One explains how you can receive it.)

The Holy Spirit wants to manifest His power through you, through the spiritual gifts He has given.

4. The Holy Spirit can manifest any of His gifts through any believer.

You have a gift given by God. That gift is your primary function in the body. It is part of your spiritual identity.

But it's also true that you can, on occasion, exercise *any* of the gifts.

All of the gifts are resident in the Holy Spirit, and He is free to manifest ANY of those gifts through you. That's why the Word says, "ALL can prophesy (I Cor. 14:26,31), ALL can speak in tongues (I Cor. 14:18, 26), ALL can teach (Heb. 5:12), All can lay hands of the sick and see them healed (Mk 16:18)."

In I Cor. 12, Paul describes how, when the church assembles in a synaxis, the Holy Spirit distributes His gifts. "To one is given a word of wisdom, to another a word of knowledge, to another faith, to another gifts of healing…"

When I read this, I picture the Holy Spirit as the dealer in a card game. When everyone has gathered, He shuffles the deck and deals out the cards.

And while every believer has their own spiritual gift, in the context of a synaxis, the Holy Spirit can manifest any gift through any believer. One person may get a prophetic word. Another has a prompting to give a message in tongues. Someone else receives the interpretation. Somebody else gets an anointing to heal the sick.

You never know who the Spirit will choose. It's like the "dancing hand" of God moving through the meeting.

That's what *manifestation* means. Manifestation comes from two Latin words, *mani,* which means *hand,* and *fest* which means *fiesta* or *festive dance.* God's manifestations are His dancing hand. When God is releasing the manifestations of the Spirit, you never know where His hand will land.

You never know when God might choose *you* to heal a sick person or give a prophetic word. You may have never prayed for a sick person in your life but as you're in the synaxis and people gather around to pray for someone who is sick, you suddenly feel prompted to pray. As you put your hand on them and pray, you feel a sensation of heat or tingling in your hand. Something is happening. And then the person says; "I think I'm healed!"

Healing has been released. Through YOU.

That doesn't mean that you have the gift of healing on a permanent basis. You have simply received a momentary anointing to heal. John Wimber described these momentary anointings as "gracelets." They are droplets of grace. On the level of a momentary anointing, you can operate in any gift.

Years ago, a woman approached Linda before church on a Sunday morning. She looked miserable. She was obviously sick. Her first words were, "Don't get too close. I'm contagious."

When she said that, the Holy Spirit's anointing fell on Linda. Linda answered, "I'm contagious too! I'm contagious with the power of God!" Without stopping to think, Linda put her hand on the woman's head and healed her.

That was a momentary anointing. Linda can't do that normally. But in a given time and place, God can manifest any gift thru any one of us.

That's why you can never say, "That's not my gift."

Some years ago, I was teaching a class at Wagner Leadership Institute in Korea. There were about 200 students present. After the afternoon session, the head of the school asked all the students to line up, and announced that I would now give a personal prophetic word to each of them.

For a moment, I panicked. I wanted to say, "Wait. I'm not a prophet, I'm a teacher."

I've seen Chuck Pierce give prophetic words to large groups like that many times, but I felt totally unqualified. I knew there were probably many students in the room that had stronger prophetic gifts than I did.

But I also knew God could release a prophetic anointing to me when I needed it. And He did. I gave a prophetic word to each student present.

So never say, "I can't do that." Move forward in faith, and the Holy Spirit will meet you.

God wants all of us to be prepared to do it all.

Learn to function in every anointing God gives.

5. It is important for every believer to discover their gifts.

God tells us that He has given every believer at least one spiritual gift. The problem is, you might not know what it is.

How do you discover your gift?

I've read a lot of books about spiritual gifts, and found that different authors suggest different ways to discover your gifts. Some of these suggestions can be very helpful. They include,

A. Examine your heart's desire. (Do you have a desire in your heart to minister in a certain way?) If you have great compassion for the sick, for example, chances are good that you might have a healing gift.

B. Pay attention to prophetic words. If you are in a church where prophetic ministry takes place, you will probably receive many prophetic words directing you to a particular kind of ministry. (These words can be helpful, but they must be tested carefully.)

C. Read books to gain understanding of the gifts. Gaining an understanding of the gifts is always helpful, and there are many good books on the subject. Peter Wagner's book, *Discover Your Spiritual Gifts* even includes a test to help point you toward your gift.

While all of these suggestions can be helpful, in the end, there's really only one way to discover your gift, and that is to actually ATTEMPT TO MINISTER.

If you see that someone is sick, you lay hands on them and pray for their healing.

If someone is discouraged or depressed, pray for them, and see if God gives you a prophetic word to encourage them.

Gifts activate in real ministry situations, and it's in the process of ministry that you discover what your gifts are.

That shouldn't be surprising. That's how you discover your gifts and talents in the natural realm also.

How do you find out if you are talented in art?

You try your hand at drawing. You take an art class.

As you try to do something artistic, you may discover that art is not "your thing."

But you may also discover that you have an incredible gift. People may start lining up to buy the works of art you produced.

But you never know till you TRY.

I played guitar for many years, and developed a moderate degree of skill. My oldest son Mike, enjoyed playing the guitar also.

But when my youngest son, Josh, was in 7th grade, I offered to show him some chords. He picked up the guitar and learned to play in just a few weeks. I was amazed. He had a natural talent that went far beyond what I could do. Within a few months, he knew everything I did, so we signed him up for guitar lessons with a professional guitarist. Six months later his guitar teacher came to me and said, "I enjoy jamming with Josh, but he already knows everything I can teach him." Josh went on to play in professional bands for a number of years. I'm still amazed at his talent.

How did Josh learn that he was gifted in the area of music? It wasn't by taking a test or reading a book.

He discovered his gift by trying. He tried to play the guitar, and his gift became obvious.

If he had never had an opportunity to try, he could have lived his whole life without discovering that he had an incredible gift to play the guitar!

That's how many Christians are with their spiritual gifts. They can have incredible gifts locked up inside them: gifts to heal, to prophesy, to work miracles. But if they never have an opportunity to *try*, they can live their whole lives never suspecting that they are gifted.

6. Functioning in the gifts involves a process of growth.

Many Christians look at the gifts as a static thing. They think they have one spiritual gift, and that's all they can do.

That's not how the Bible describes gifts. The Bible describes the functioning of the gifts as a process of growth. You may have one gift, but that gift can increase in power as you use it. You can also gain additional gifts. As a matter of fact, the Word commands us to *seek* additional gifts!

Notice some of the instructions God gives us about the gifts:

God instructs us to stir up and exercise the gifts we have. I Tim. 4:11 warns us not to *neglect* our spiritual gift. Don't let it lie dormant.

II Tim:1:6 exhorts us to *stir up* our gift (NKJV), to fan it into flames! (NIV) The picture here is of a fire that has been reduced to glowing embers. There is still life present, but it is very weak. But stirring those embers causes them to erupt in flames. Your spiritual gift may seem to be weak, operating at a very low level. But if you stir that gift up, it can operate in great power.

God instructs us to pray for and seek additional gifts. There's a basic biblical principle: If you are faithful with what you've been given, you will be given more. It's important to discover and use the gift God has given you, but God doesn't want you to be satisfied with just one! He wants you to desire more!

God tells us to seek greater gifts. (I Cor. 12:31)

He says, if you minister in tongues, pray for also for the gift of interpretation. (I Cor 14:31)

He urges us to seek *all* the spiritual gifts, but especially the gift of prophecy. (I Cor 14:1)

Amazingly, God tells us to *COVET* the gift of prophecy. (I Cor 14:39 KJV). That's the only thing in the world God wants you to covet! To covet anything else is sin. But to *fail* to covet prophecy is disobedience.

One way to receive an additional gift is through the process of impartation. The Bible teaches that spiritual gifts can be imparted from one believer to another, often by the laying on of hands. Notice the following passages:

Numbers 11 – When the 70 elders met with Moses, God took of the Spirit that was on Moses and put it on them. The result was, they began to prophesy.

I Samuel 10 – When Saul came into contact with a group of prophets, he "caught" what they had. He began to prophesy.

Romans 1:11 – Paul describes his desire to visit Rome, in order that he might impart a spiritual gift to the Romans.

I Timothy 4:14 – Timothy had a spiritual gift imparted to him when a group of elders laid hands on him and prophesied over him.

II Timothy 1:6 – Speaks of a gift imparted through Paul's hands.

Years ago, I attended John Wimber's Power Evangelism conference in Birmingham, Alabama. At the time, the ministries of the Holy Spirit were still new to me, but I was eager to learn.

One gift I had been praying for and seeking was the gift of healing. I had seen God use me in healing several times, but I felt I was still at a kindergarten level when it came to healing ministry.

I had seen that many who operated in healing also operated in a gift called, "Word of Knowledge." A word of knowledge often is manifested in a unique way. The person praying for healing can actually feel the pain the other person is feeling, allowing him to pray very specifically. So I began to pray for the word of knowledge.

At the Power Evangelism conference, John Wimber described how gifts can be imparted from one believer to another. At the end of the session, he said, "If you have a gift that you've been praying for, raise your hand and one of our ministry team members will come and impart that gift to you."

I immediately put my hand up.

A short time later, a member of the ministry team came over and asked what gift I was praying for.

I told him, "Word of Knowledge."

At that point, the ministry team member did something very strange. He reached out his hand, touched me lightly in the forehead, and said, "Okay, you've got word of knowledge."

I was a little offended. He didn't say a long prayer or pray in tongues. He just said, "Okay, you've got word of knowledge."

I felt like he had not taken my request seriously.

But then he asked, "Did you feel anything happen when I touched your head?"

And I suddenly realized that I *did* feel something. The moment he touched my head, my right ear closed up. It became painful and felt like it was stuffed with cotton. I also realized that my hearing in that ear had decreased.

When I shared what I was feeling, my friend Brock, who had come to the conference with me and was standing right next to me, got excited.

"That's ME!" He exclaimed. "My right ear has felt like that for the last week."

I realized that I had just experienced a word of knowledge. My prayer for that gift was answered!

And the gift has not gone away. Since that day, any time I'm prompted to ask for a word of knowledge, I get one. It's now a gift I feel very comfortable using.

That should be a normal experience for every Christian. We should be constantly gaining proficiency in more and more of the Holy Spirit's gifts so we can be more and more effective in serving Jesus.

There's one more thing we need to know about spiritual gifts. If you want to DISCOVER your gift, or DEVELOP your gift, or INCREASE your gifts, you need one thing above all else: A GROWTH ENVIRONMENT.

I believe that's what was on Jesus' heart when He instructed the apostles on setting up the early church. He had the apostles establish the early church as a perfect growth environment for the gifts of the Spirit.

Endnotes

1	Gibbon, Edward, *The Decline and Fall of the Roman Empire.* Vol. I. (New York, NY: The Modern Library), As quoted in Jackson, Wayne. "A Historian's Assessment of Ancient Christianity." <https://www.christiancourier.com/articles/733-historians-assessment-of-ancient-christianity-a> [7-31-2019].

16

A Growth Environment For the Gifts

In the early church, every believer was taught about the gifts and witnessed the gifts in operation, but perhaps even more importantly, they also had an opportunity to exercise their gifts every week.

We need that in the church today.

You will rarely find someone who gets baptized in the Spirit and immediately begins to operate in a gift with great proficiency. Proficiency in the gifts takes time. It takes growth. People who are learning to exercise gifts will make mistakes. This is true for all of the gifts, whether prophecy, teaching, healing, etc.

To "grow a church" full of people who function with maturity in the gifts, the members must be cared for and nurtured. They must be given opportunities to try to exercise the gifts without fear of rejection. If they do something wrong, or are ministering in a way that is harmful, they must be gently corrected, and encouraged to try again.

Unfortunately, most churches today do not provide an environment that is conducive for growth in the gifts. In most church activities, only one or two people have any opportunity to speak or minister, and it's usually those who have already shown themselves to be proficient in ministry.

That's why a meeting like a synaxis is important. In a synaxis, everyone is free to try.

"When you come together, *everyone* has a song, or a word of instruction, or a revelation, a tongue or an interpretation."

In a synaxis, if you think you have a prophetic word, you are free to give it. You are among friends. These are people who know you and are committed to you. It's okay to try. (If you think you have a word from God, you don't have to proudly boast, "Thus says the Lord!" Especially when you are just beginning, it's probably better to speak with humility, "I think I hear the Lord saying…") That leaves you open for gentle correction if you are wrong. A synaxis is a safe place to learn how your gift functions.

Paul gives several instructions for exercising the gifts in a synaxis….

If anyone speaks in a tongue, two--or at the most three--should speak, one at a time, and someone must interpret. If there is no interpreter, the speaker should keep quiet in the church and speak to himself and God.

Two or three prophets should speak, and the others should weigh carefully what is said. And if a revelation comes to someone who is sitting down, the first speaker should stop. For you can all prophesy in turn so that everyone may be instructed and encouraged." -I Cor. 14:26-31

So EVERYONE at this meeting was encouraged to participate. Each one could prophecy, speak in tongues, give a teaching, etc.

People were free to respond as the Spirit led them. One might give a brief message in a tongue (14:27). If a tongue was given, the group would wait for the interpretation. If there was no one present who could give an interpretation, there would be no more messages in tongues at that meeting. (Of course, they were still free to pray in tongues as a personal prayer language.) If an interpretation was given, others could bring a tongues message, although not more than three in any one meeting (14:27-28).

Those who received revelation from God (a prophecy, a vision, a word of knowledge) would be free to share it. When something was said, it would be tested by the others there (14:29). If what was said "bore witness" with the others as a valid word from God, they would all confirm it by answering "Amen" (14:16). This provided immediate feedback for the person who shared.

The ministry all had to be done in an orderly way. They were careful not to interrupt each other (14:30-32).

From the description of the gathering in I Cor. 12, it is clear that other things also took place at this meeting. If one was sick, others might gather around and lay their hands on him and pray for healing. If one had a need, the others would pray in faith for God to work.

This kind of meeting was the norm in the early church. It provided a setting where people could learn to recognize the voice of God, and learn to operate in His anointings. I believe it is vital for the church today to have times where this kind of growth environment is created.

It's in that kind of environment that gifts can flourish.

It's like learning to ride a bike!

When I teach on the gifts, I often ask, "How did you learn to ride a bike?"

Did you study blueprints to learn how to bicycles are made? Did you read books about bike riding? Did you sit in a classroom and listen to a lecture about how to ride a book?

No!

You could do all those things and you still won't know how to ride a bike!

To learn to ride a bike you need 2 things: you need a bike to practice on and you need someone you trust to help you get started. And if you have those 2 things you can learn to ride a bike very quickly.

The same thing is true with your spiritual gift. You will not learn your spiritual gift by taking a class. You will not learn your spiritual gift by reading a book. You will not learn your spiritual gift by going to church on a Sunday morning.

To learn your spiritual gift; you need two things: You need an opportunity to minister, and you need someone you trust to show your how. "Put this hand here and pray like this…"

When you have those two things, your gift will flourish. That's what I call a growth environment.

That's what every member of the early church experienced from day one. They went to the celebration where their faith was strengthened, then they came to the synaxis where they were given an opportunity to try for themselves. There were leaders present to give instruction, correction, and encouragement.

That's what every believer needs today. You need a celebration to build your faith but you also need a Synaxis to release your gift. Within the context of those two kinds of meetings the church's 5-fold ministers could equip every believer to do the works of Jesus.

In a typical church today, most Christians NEVER have an opportunity to exercise their gift! (I'm convinced that the main reason most Christians never discover their gifts is that they've never spent time in situations where spiritual gifts can operate.)

Years ago, we had a young woman named Rachel in the church. When the subject of prophecy came up, Rachel always said, "I can't do that. Other people get prophetic words, words of knowledge, and visions. But I can't hear God."

Then Rachel went with us to a conference in another city. As part of the conference, Glory of Zion provided a prophetic team to do prophetic ministry for anyone who desired it. We would have four or five "prophetic ministers" sitting in a semi-circle. People would come in one-at-a-time and sit across from the team members, then each team member would share any prophetic revelation they sensed. (This kind of ministry is often called a prophetic presbytery.)

When our group got to the conference, we said, "Rachel, why don't you sit in with the prophetic team as they minister?"

She immediately said, "But I'm not prophetic!"

We said, "Just give it a try."

So Rachel sat in with the team, as one person after another came in and sat down, expecting to receive a prophetic word. As she sat there, listening to the others prophesy, Rachel suddenly began hear what God was saying also! By the end of the day, Rachael had received prophetic words, words of knowledge, and amazing visions. She was so excited! She had heard God!

Rachel had found a growth environment where her prophetic gift could be released.

Very often, your spiritual gifts will not activate until you find yourself in a ministry situation.

Testimony: Developing the Gift of Prophecy

Let me give an example of equipping the saints to minister.

In the mid-1980s, I went with some friends to a church in the nearby city of Arlington, Texas to hear a prophet.

I had never heard a prophet before, and was somewhat surprised. The man didn't stand up and give a message. Instead, he started picking people out of the congregation and giving them prophetic words.

I WAS AMAZED!

I could tell by people's response that he was "reading their mail."

I thought, "How does he do that?"

At the time, prophetic ministry was not common, at least in our circles.

But over the next few years we got to know some prophets. Chuck Pierce is an apostle, but he is also a prophet. Chuck's brother Keith is also a prophet. Barbara Wentroble is both a prophet and an apostle.

We started having prophetic conferences, prophetic training weekends, and schools of the prophets.

Our people could hear examples of mature prophets at our worship celebrations, and received much teaching about prophecy. But the most important thing we did was establish what I like to call a "prophetic synaxis."

In the early 90s, Chuck Pierce initiated regular times of what he called *corporate prophetic intercession*. They were designed to press us forward against the demonic resistance that had been endemic in our region, but they also

A Growth Environment for the Gifts

functioned as a synaxis for prophetic gifts.

We've held regular prophetic intercession meetings for over twenty years now. The result has been that the powers of darkness have been driven back, and the Kingdom advanced. We held these prophetic intercession meetings at least once a week, and in some seasons, daily. For more than a year, we had 100+ people show up at 5:15 every morning to intercede.

At these meetings, the leader sets a direction, and a worship team brings us into God's presence, but everyone is encouraged to participate. Everyone can declare what they sense the Spirit saying. If correction is necessary, it's usually given gently, or in private.

These prophetic intercession meetings provided a growth environment for gifts of prophecy, and in that context, people developed in the prophetic gifts very rapidly.

The result is that we now have hundreds of people who can effectively prophesy. Prophecy has become *common* at Glory of Zion. I can look around in our church and point out dozens of people who can do what that man in Arlington did!

This was really brought home to me earlier this year when Chuck announced that we would host a week-long Prophetic Hotline, where people from all over the world could call in and get a free prophetic word. During that week we had ten phone lines available from 6 am to 6 pm every day, and they were continually BUSY. When one call ended, another would already be waiting on hold.

To answer the phones, we scheduled more than 200 volunteers from the church to serve in shifts to give people prophetic words. It struck me that those 200 people were doing exactly what that prophet in Arlington had done!

(If you can prophesy to a stranger on the phone, they can prophesy anywhere.)

We received many, many testimonies of how accurate the prophetic words were. That told me we had been successful in EQUIPPING the saints to prophecy. And these people don't just prophesy on the phone. We've had people prophesy in their office, in their classroom, in their neighborhoods, and at the grocery store. We've seen people saved through prophetic words.

That's what happens when there is a growth environment for the gifts.

Think of the implications this has for the church.

In chapter 12, I painted a picture of the believers in an average pastoral church today. They faithfully come to church every week, but have no idea that God has given them a spiritual gift. They've never been instructed in the gifts, or been given an opportunity to exercise them.

To understand the importance of a synaxis, I'd like us to look at that picture in more detail.

The Barna Research Group tells us that the average size of a Protestant church in America is about 90 members.[1] Since there are 9 ministry gifts, let's assume that among those 90 members, we might find 10 people with each of the gifts. (I'm oversimplifying for the sake of argument.)

So in that congregation, there could be ten people with the gift of prophecy, ten people with a gift of faith, ten with a gift of miracles, and ten with a gift to heal the sick.

In that church, the 10 "healers" show up at church every Sunday. They sing some songs, hear a sermon, give an offering, and go home, thinking they have made God happy by coming to church.

But they are never built up in their faith for healing. They are not taught to lay hands on the sick. They are never given opportunity to pray for the sick.

With no opportunity to try, they never discover their gifts. They live their whole life with no idea they have a healing gift.

Now picture what would have happened in a first century synaxis. An average synaxis might have only 20 people meeting in a living room. Chances are very good that at least two people in that group are gifted to heal. Two others have the gift of faith. Two more have the gift of miracles.

But these believers have been taught about healing. They have witnessed miracles and dramatic healings take place. Their faith has been built up.

Every week they are encouraged to exercise their gifts. Many weeks there are sick people present in their group who need prayer.

They begin to see people healed. Their faith increases even more. Healings and miracles happen with more and more frequency. They can't wait to get to the synaxis each week to see what God will do.

Now comes the test. A family in the community is in crisis. Their child is sick and dying, and the doctors can offer no hope. While not Christians, the family is desperate. They decide to see if God can help them.

If that family comes to a typical 21st century pastoral church, what do you imagine would happen? If they share their need, the pastor might pray a beautiful, religious-sounding prayer, and offer words of comfort. Lots of people may gather around them to show compassion and give them hugs. But in the end, their daughter is not healed.

But suppose that family lived back in the first century, and dropped in at a nearby synaxis. According to the testimony of both Scripture and history, they would likely come away with more than just compassion and comfort. They would have a very good chance of seeing a demonstration of the power of God. Their daughter would be healed, and the whole family saved!

Endnotes

1   The Barna research group estimates the average Protestant church size in America to be 89 adults. (statistic is the attendance on an average weekend.) <https://www.barna.com/research/small-churches-struggle-to-grow-because-of-the-people-they-attract/> [7-14-2019].

17

The Apostolic Church and the Last-Days Revival
Life in a Supernatural Church.

God never intended Church to have one person minister while everybody else just came and watched. God wants all of us to minister. That's what happened in the New Testament:

In Acts 8, they all went and preached.

In Mark 16, we're told that all can heal. All can cast out demons.

In John 14, we're told that all who believe in Jesus can do the works Jesus did.

In I Corinthians 14, we're told that all can prophesy.

In Hebrews 5, we're told that all should be teaching.

God wants you to learn to do the things that Jesus did. To put it bluntly; you have a call from God to minister!

That's part of why you were created, and you will only find fulfillment in life when you do what God created you to do.

God wants us to gain a new vision of our call as Christians. If you know Jesus, you are not called to just be a loyal church member who attends church every week until you die and go to heaven.

God called you to *minister*. The church's job is to equip you to do that. That's God's plan for the church.

When the church equips every believer to minister, incredible things start to happen. I love Acts chapter 8. We're told that after Steven was martyred, great persecution broke out against the church in Jerusalem, and all accept the apostles were scattered throughout Judea and Samaria.

The church is now several years old. By this time, many estimate the church had grown to 20,000 members. Those temple courts were getting pretty crowded and the Jewish religious leaders were getting concerned. This "*Yeshua* Movement" seemed to be taking over. So persecution began to rise.

To avoid the persecution; everybody but the apostles left town. The members of the church were scattered across the countryside. We think; "Oh, those poor scattered sheep. They fled Jerusalem, while the apostles stayed behind. This could be a disaster. *The church could be destroyed!*"

But look at what those poor scattered sheep did. Acts 8 tells us, "Those who had been scattered preached the Word wherever they went." *Those poor sheep went out and preached!*

"With shrieks evil spirits came out of many and many paralytics and cripples were healed." *Those poor scattered sheep went all through the countryside performing miracles!*

By Acts chapter 9, we're told, "the Church throughout Judea and Samaria and Galilee enjoyed a time of peace it was strengthened and grew in number living in the fear of the Lord." *Those poor scattered sheep went out and planted strong, healthy churches wherever they went!*

How do we account for this?

As the members of the Jerusalem church met from house to house in synaxis, every one of them learned how to heal the sick, prophesy, teach, drive out demons, and all the rest.

Because they had learned how to minister, when they fled Jerusalem it was the most natural thing in the world for them to minister wherever they went.

And so; they went all over the territory doing the works of Jesus. The result was; people got saved and the church advanced. That was God's PLAN for His church!

The world was changed!

The church spread everywhere!

Within 67 years the early church took the Gospel to the entire known world. A synaxis would be planted in a city and quickly multiply. Soon their number grew to 30 or 40,000 Christians.

That's what the early church was like.

That is the church that *WAS*.

But it is also the church that *WILL BE*.

God is restoring His Church. God has restored celebration. For centuries church had been a sad, mournful place, mired in religion and unbelief. But now all over the world the church is learning the power of joyful celebration.

At Glory of Zion we have praise celebrations every Sunday morning. People gather from all over the world for conferences and join in the celebration. Whether you join us live or by webcast you can join in and faith is increased.

But God is also restoring the synaxis—smaller groups usually meeting in a living room. At Glory of Zion we have Houses of Zion, house churches, thousands of them all over the world. Believers are finding opportunities to practice their gifts.

Where is all of this headed?

I believe the end result will be FULL RESTORATION.

Smith Wigglesworth prophecy

I'd like to share a prophetic word given by the great Pentecostal preacher, Smith Wigglesworth to his friend, Lester Sumrall in 1939, when they met for the last time.

With tears rolling down his face Smith cried, "I probably won't see you again. My job is almost finished." Then he cried, "I see it, I see it."

Lester Sumrall asked, "What do you see?"

He said, "I see a healing revival coming right after World War II. It'll be so easy to get people healed. I see it. I see it. I won't be here for it, but you will be."

That's exactly what happened. The 1940s and 50s, a great move of healing evangelism swept the world.

But Wigglesworth continued to prophesy, "I see another one, I see people of all different denominations being filled with the Holy Ghost."

That was the Charismatic Movement. In the 60s the Spirit invaded mainline denominations. In the 80's it even spread to Evangelical churches.

Then he continued, "I see another move of God. I see auditoriums full of people, coming with notebooks. There will be a wave of teaching on faith and healing."

We saw that in the 70's. It was a decade of great Charismatic teaching conferences, with teachers like Derek Prince, and the Word of Faith movement.

But Wigglesworth continued, "After that, after the third wave," he started sobbing. "I see THE LAST DAY REVIVAL that's going to usher in the precious fruit of the earth!

"It will be the greatest revival this world has ever seen. It's going to be a wave of the GIFTS OF THE SPIRIT!

"The MINISTRY GIFTS will be flowing on this planet earth. I see hospitals being emptied out, and they will bring the sick to churches where they allow the Holy Ghost to move."[1]

I believe that's where the church is heading now.

The apostolic Movement was birthed to re-establish 5-fold ministry, so God's people can again be equipped to minister.

The new wineskin has now been prepared.

We are about see the church function once again in the power of the early church. God's people will use their gifts to heal the sick, drive out demons, and perform miracles wherever they go. And when *that* happens, it will change the world.

It has already begun.

Everything is about to change!

The Apostolic Church is Advancing!

Endnotes

1   <https://www.charismanews.com/opinion/the-flaming-herald/74919-smith-wigglesworth-offers-great-encouragement-warning-for-the-coming-days> [7-12-2019].

Appendix I

How to Be Baptized in the Holy Spirit

NOTE: This appendix contains material from my book, Experiencing the Spirit, which is available at Glory of Zion.org, and Amazon.com. Experiencing the Spirit is recommended for anyone seeking to walk in the power of the Holy Spirit.

In my book, *Experiencing the Spirit*, I share the account of the first time I ever prayed for someone to be baptized in the Holy Spirit…

"You've got to help me." the voice on the phone pleaded, "There's got to be more to the Christian life than what I'm experiencing. If this is all there is, I don't want it anymore." He paused a moment, then continued almost apologetically, "I don't even know why I'm calling you, but as I've prayed I just had a feeling that you would have an answer for me."

The speaker on the phone had been one of my best friends during my seminary years. Although not a seminary student himself, Ben was one of the most knowledgeable Christians I knew. A highly intelligent man, the shelves in his living room were lined with the works of the great Protestant theologians.

Ben liked nothing better than to argue some obscure theological point, and he had the knowledge to do it well. But he was not calling me to argue theology this time. He had reached a point in his life where an "intellectual" faith no longer satisfied. He sensed there was a reality to the Christian life that went beyond knowing the right doctrines, and he was desperate to find it.

Although he lived in a city less than an hour's drive from mine, I had not seen Ben for several years, so I was surprised when he chose to call me for help in this time of desperation. What Ben had no way of knowing was that the Holy Spirit had done a major work of renewal in my life less than a year earlier.

Ben and I set up a time to meet and I shared with him my testimony of how the Spirit of God had recently worked in my life.

Ben responded like a little child in a candy store. He wanted to experience the empowering of the Spirit himself. I shared with him what little I knew about the work of the Spirit, and he was ready for me to pray for him to be filled.

I suggested that he confess any known sins, we sang a few praise songs, and as he sat on the couch in his living room, I laid my hand on his head and prayed for him to be filled with the Spirit. We sat there in silence for a few moments, and absolutely nothing happened.

I could tell Ben was really disappointed, and frankly, I was also. I had seen the Spirit of God do a great work in my life and I hoped God would do something similar for Ben.

We talked for a while longer and I got up to leave. As we stood at the door, I experienced a strange sensation. I sensed in my spirit that the Holy Spirit of God had come and was "resting" on Ben, ready to do something.

Appendix I

Awkwardly, I said, "Ben, I sense the Holy Spirit on you right now. I think we need to go back and pray one more time."

We went back into his living room and he again sat down on his couch. Once again, I laid my hand on his head and asked the Holy Spirit to come and fill Ben.

This time something began to happen. Ben suddenly began to breathe very deeply and tremble all over. He leaned back on the couch and seemed to go into a kind of trance. From time to time he would groan or mumble a prayer like, "Oh, dear Jesus."

This went on for twenty minutes, and to be honest, I was a little frightened. First of all, this was totally out of character for Ben. Ben was an intellectual. I had never known him to be an emotionally demonstrative person.

Secondly, I had never personally experienced or even seen anything like this before. . . ever! Nothing like this had happened to me when the Spirit of God touched me. I honestly worried that Ben was having some kind of breakdown. My one consolation was that I kept hearing the Spirit of God telling me, "It's all right. This is Me."

When Ben finally "came out of it" he was so excited. He said that it had felt like the Spirit of God was peeling away layer after layer, penetrating down into his innermost being and changing him. It was the most wonderful thing he had ever experienced.

Then Ben began to prophesy. As we sat there together, the Holy Spirit began to tell him things he had no way of knowing. Ben prophesied things about me and about my ministry that were

100% accurate. I had never witnessed anything like it before.

Ben's experience with the Holy Spirit was not a cure-all. Ben has gone through some difficult times since this experience. But it has changed him. Anyone who knew Ben before will testify that in many ways he is now a different person. He has had an experiential encounter with the Spirit of the Living God. The power of God has been poured out upon him, and the supernatural gifts of the Spirit have begun to operate in his life. He will never be the same.

Since that evening in Ben's living room, I have prayed for many, many people to receive the empowering of the Holy Spirit. Many have had dramatic experiences. Some have just felt a sense of peace and the presence of the Spirit. Some have spoken in tongues. A few have prophesied. But for almost all, the outcome was a major transformation of life brought about by the empowering Spirit of God. In this appendix we will look at some Biblical principles about receiving the Spirit's empowering.

Key Facts About Empowering

1. Empowering is a discernable experience.

The empowering of the Spirit is not something you have to "take by faith." It is experiential. When the Spirit comes upon you, you KNOW something has happened. It is evident to you, and it is often evident to others around you.

In Acts chapter eight when Philip preached in Samaria, many Samaritans were saved. It was obvious to Philip, however, that the Holy Spirit had not yet "come upon" any of them (Acts 8:16). This indicates that there were outward signs Philip looked for to see if a person had received the Spirit's empowering.

When word arrived in Jerusalem that the Samaritans had been saved but not empowered, the Jerusalem church sent Peter and John to lay hands on the Samaritans. Verses 18-19 indicate that as Peter and John laid hands on these Samaritans, something happened. They had a definite and observable experience with the Spirit.

What the Samaritans experienced was so dramatic that a man named Simon, a magician, offered Peter and John money to teach him how to do it. This passage doesn't say what the outward signs were, but it was impressive enough that a professional magician was willing to pay money to learn it. I've known some magicians, and believe me, they don't offer money for a trick unless it's impressive.

These Samaritan Christians, like my friend Ben and many others in the Bible, had an experiential encounter with the Spirit of God.

Many people get very uncomfortable when we talk about experiences with God. Some have even been taught to fear experiences. But it's not wrong to want to experience the One who loved you and gave His life for you. As we saw in chapter one, the men and women of the Bible did not hesitate to seek experiences with God. David and the other Psalmists longed to experience God's presence. Much of the Bible is a record of the experiences people had with God.

The Bible consistently teaches that the empowering of the Spirit is experiential. When the power and presence of the Holy Spirit is manifested in the life of a believer, discernable changes take place.

Sometimes the evidence of empowering is the release of a spiritual gift. As you read through the Bible, you find that about 80% of the time the empowering of the Spirit is accompanied by the person either speaking in tongues or prophesying.

Augustine wrote that, in the early church, the norm was when a person received the Spirit he spoke in other tongues. Augustine also said, however, that this was not always the case.

This is still true today. If a person has not been taught against speaking in tongues, the release of tongues is a normal and typical response to the Spirit's empowering. I personally believe that every believer who is empowered by the Spirit has the capacity to pray in tongues. I also believe that, for a number of reasons, not everyone does.

I have known several people who received a very powerful anointing from the Spirit and began to function in such gifts as prophecy and healing, yet did not receive a release to pray in tongues until many months later. There are a number of Biblical examples of people filled with the Spirit without an immediate release of tongues.

I think the Spirit also demonstrates His empowering presence in a number of other ways. Sometimes, as I pray for people to be empowered by the Spirit, there is the sensation of a mantle of heat coming down upon them. Sometimes they have felt overwhelmed by waves of power. Sometimes there is an unexplainable weeping, trembling, or even a violent shaking. Sometimes they simply fall over unconscious. Those are all Biblical "calling cards" of the Spirit. They are His way of saying: "I'm here now to empower you."

While the evidences of the Spirit's presence may differ from one occasion to another, I believe the empowering is always experiential.

2. Empowering Is Sudden

In His indwelling ministry, the Holy Spirit works through a gradual process to mature us. It is a growth process. It takes a long time to form the character of Christ in us.

In His empowering ministry, the Spirit works through a sudden outpouring, (a baptism, an inundation with His presence), to drench us with His power.

If you have been at the ocean and had a big wave come and crash down on you, you know what it means to be inundated. That is the kind of language the Bible uses to describe empowering. It doesn't take a long time. It's just there.

That's why a very young Christian can sometimes exercise great power. A brand new Christian who has received the Spirit's empowering may be able to receive words from the Lord, pray for the sick and see them healed, speak with other tongues, and prophesy to reveal the secrets of men's hearts. These things are possible because the exercise of God's power is not dependent on growth. God's power is freely given to any of His children who truly desire and seek it.

One reason many Christians never experience God's power is that they never seek it. Some have been taught that it is wrong to seek God's power. They talk as though it would be presumptuous to ask God for it. This could not be further from the truth. In I Cor. 12-14 we are told to earnestly desire the gifts and power of God. The apostle Paul did not hesitate to yearn for more of this power. He said that he suffered great hardships so that he could more fully know "the power of His resurrection" (Phil 3:10). It is not "more spiritual" to live a powerless Christian life. God wants His people to have His power and He is willing to pour it out on all who will seek it.

3. Empowering Must Be Maintained

It's important to notice that the empowering of the Spirit is not a "once for all" occurrence. After your initial inundation by the Spirit, there need to be subsequent times of filling, and additional anointings of the Spirit for specific purposes. We see that Peter and the other apostles were filled with God's power in Acts 2, but then they prayed again and were filled again in Acts 4.

The New Testament also seems to indicate there are different levels of empowering. Your initial empowering may not give you a great deal of power, but as you keep going back to God for more and faithfully use what He gives, you will increase your capacity to function in the power of God.

Don't be satisfied with one experience of empowering. Keep going back to the Lord and receiving more.

The Results of Empowering

When people receive the empowering of the Spirit, it is normal that there be some definite changes in their lives. Some of the things that often occur include:

1. A New Desire for Praise and Worship (Eph. 5:18-20)

When the Holy Spirit invaded my life back in 1983, one of the first changes I noticed was the release of praise to God. I had gone through a time of deep depression when, in response to a friend's prayer, the Holy Spirit invaded our house, literally overnight. When I awoke the next morning, praise songs were filling my mind. All through the day, almost like "background music," there was a constant flow of praise to Jesus. It bubbled up from my spirit with no conscious effort on my part. There was a richness, satisfaction and joy in praising Jesus that I had never felt in anything else. As I drifted off to sleep that night my spirit was still overflowing with joyful praise. In the weeks that followed, I picked up my guitar that I hadn't played in years and God began to give me new songs. Sometimes I would be reading a passage of scripture, and I would "hear" a tune that went with it. I would sit with Him for hours and sing songs of love and praise to Jesus. This lasted literally for months.

Not everyone has that experience when the Spirit comes upon them, but it's not unusual. That's why Ephesians five says, "be filled with the Spirit, singing to one another in psalms ..."

The empowering of the Spirit releases a river of praise in our Spirits. That's why Charismatic and Pentecostal churches usually put such a strong emphasis on praise and worship. Before our church was invaded by the Spirit we were satisfied with two or three hymns on Sunday morning, and most people seemed impatient with that. Now we have over an hour of praise and worship every Sunday and nobody wants to stop. The presence of the Spirit gives us a desire for intimacy with God that can only be satisfied in praise and worship.

2. Supernatural Manifestations (Gifts - I Cor. 12)

When a person is empowered by the Spirit, they usually experience the release of tongues or prophecy. Those two manifestations of the Spirit are just the starting point, however. I believe once an individual is filled with the Spirit they have the capacity to function in any of the gifts of the Spirit described in

A TRIUMPHANT KINGDOM

I Cor. 12.

3. Spiritual Discernment, Perception

When you are empowered by the Spirit, you gain discernment and perception in the spiritual realm. Many testify that when they are filled with the Spirit, they feel like a blind man whose eyes have just been opened. They are suddenly aware of a new level of Spiritual reality.

4. A New Level of Warfare (Eph. 6)

When you are empowered by the Spirit, you become much more of a threat to Satan's kingdom, and consequently find yourself catapulted into a new level of warfare. My friend, John Dickson, says the real sign of the baptism of the Holy Spirit is not tongues, but trouble. That's because most people experience an increased level of spiritual attack for several months after the Spirit's filling.

This season of Spiritual attack lasts until we recognize what it is and learn to put on our spiritual armor as described in Eph 6. By way of encouragement, we should note that it is not God's will for you to walk through this period in defeat, under the oppression of the enemy. He has provided all you need to walk in continual triumph, but you do need to take His provision seriously.

5. A New Ability in Ministry (Acts 1:8)

The whole purpose of the Spirit's empowering is to equip you to minister. It is designed to give you the ability to change individual lives through the power of God and to disciple the nations.

Appendix I

Acts 1:8 Promises: "You will receive power. . . AND YOU WILL BE MY WITNESSES." THAT'S why we need the empowering of the Spirit. If all we needed to do was sit in church and sing some nice songs, we wouldn't need empowering. But God has given us a job to do. We have a world to win. We have territory to take back from the enemy. There are lives to be set free from Satan's bondage. . . . and to do that we need His power.

It is possible to be a mature Christian and allow the indwelling Spirit to produce His character in your life, but to know very little of His power. In Biblical times, this was true of the church at Thessalonica.

When Paul wrote to them in I Thessalonians, he complemented them on their maturity and their walk with the Lord. He also expressed a concern, however. In I Thess. 5:19-21 he warned them, "Do not put out the Spirit's fire. Do not treat prophecies with contempt. Test everything. Hold on to the good."

The Thessalonians knew the Spirit's indwelling. They had become mature. The character of Jesus was being formed in them. But the display of the Spirit's power made them uncomfortable.

They saw that when the Spirit began working in power there was often some confusion. (It takes time for people to learn to function in God's gifts with maturity.) The Thessalonians wanted to take the easy way out. They wanted to forbid prophecy, and focus on the more "orderly" and "acceptable" activities of learning the Word and growing to maturity.

Paul warned them not to grieve the Spirit by rejecting His manifestations. God doesn't want you to choose between maturity and power. He wants you to have both.

He wants you to repent, submit, and feed on the Word. He wants you

A TRIUMPHANT KINGDOM

to grow to maturity. But He also wants to equip you to function in His power.

Receiving His Power

While most Christians agree that it is important to be empowered by the Spirit there is a great diversity of opinion on the best way to receive that power.

Some are empowered without seeking it. When I was "baptized" in the Spirit's power I had not sought it. I wasn't even sure I wanted it. I received it by the sovereign grace of God. I believe something similar happened in the New Testament with Cornelius. Cornelius and his friends were not seeking an experience with the Spirit; they just wanted to know the Lord. But as Peter presented the gospel and faith stirred in their hearts, the Spirit of God fell upon them in power and they spoke with other tongues, just as the apostles did at Pentecost.

While there are some today that experience the Spirit's power without seeking it, the Bible makes it clear that these are the exception. In most cases the empowering of the Spirit must be sought. God wants us to desire His Spirit and pray for His fullness.

Different groups have taken different approaches to seeking the Spirit's power. Dr. Garnet Pike, a Pentecostal theologian, has written one of the best books ever written on receiving the Spirit's power. In this book *Receiving the Promise of the Father*, Dr. Pike describes how different groups attempt to bring men and women into the empowering experience.

Dr. Pike characterizes the approach of classical Pentecostalism as "tarrying" for the Spirit's power. In this method, the individual seeking "the baptism" is surrounded by a group of people who are loudly praying in tongues and praising God, usually accompanied by loud music. Emotions are stirred and much zeal is evident. In many cases, however, there is little understanding, and many go away discouraged.

In contrast to this, Dr. Pike describes an approach typical of many in the Charismatic movement. The method used by many Charismatics involves "teaching" the seeker to speak in tongues. This is sometimes accomplished by having the seeker repeat a phrase over and over while others cluster around and pray in tongues. "Sometimes unique expressions that sounded like 'shondalai' or 'look at my tie' or 'should have bought a Honda.' were spoken. The speaking pace was quickened until the counselor would say, 'You got it.'"[1]

To these approaches we might add the approach often used in the Vineyard and "Third Wave" churches. In the Third Wave approach, the Spirit's power is received by standing or sitting very still while someone prays, "Come Holy Spirit."

In recent years much of the church has experienced some version of the "Toronto blessing" style of renewal. In these services the key is laying on the floor—doing "carpet time"—long enough to "soak" in the power of the Spirit.

While some of these methods seem strange, the fact is that many godly believers have had life-changing experiences with the Spirit in each of these ways. That's because the issue in receiving God's power is not the outward form, method, or style of ministry, but a heart that yearns after the Lord and is hungry to receive His power. If you meet these criteria, and seek it persistently, you will experience the Spirit's empowering.

Keys to Receiving

While the Bible never gives a set formula for receiving the Spirit's power, a study of the Word reveals two key elements that are usually present. The first element is the Prayer of Faith.

1. Empowered Through Prayer

The first, and most crucial step in being empowered is PRAYER. The Biblical norm is to pray to be empowered by the Spirit. In Luke 11:13, Jesus speaks of the empowering ministry of the Spirit and tells us that the Father gives the Spirit to those who ask.

The empowering of the Spirit usually comes in response to prayer. In Acts chapter one we find the apostles "joined together constantly in prayer" (Acts 1:14). The result was "they were all filled with the Holy Spirit" (Acts 2:4).

In Acts chapter four we read that the disciples "raised their voices together in prayer to God" (Acts 4:24). The result was "they were all filled with the Holy Spirit" (Acts 4:31).

The prayer that releases the Spirit's power is not just a repetition of words, but a conscious expression of faith in God's willingness and desire to give you His power (Gal. 3:5). One expression of this faith is the willingness to persevere, to continue seeking until you have received (Luke 11:5-13). Like my friend Ben, many are not filled the first time they ask for it, but if they keep on seeking they will receive.

2. Empowered Through Impartation

Appendix I

The second key to receiving the Spirit's power is impartation, usually through the laying on of hands. The Spirit's power can come directly from God in response to prayer, but on most occasions God chooses to give, or impart His power through another believer.

The Apostle Paul had a dramatic conversion experience on the Damascus road when he encountered the glorified Jesus. But Paul was not empowered by the Spirit until another believer, Ananias, came and laid hands on him, praying for the Spirit to fill him. Both the Old and New Testaments show that the power of the Spirit is often received in this way. (See Acts 8:14-17 and Acts 9:11-17 for two examples.)

This pattern is still true today. God gives His people the privilege of IMPARTING the fullness of His Spirit by the laying on of hands. Hebrews chapter six identifies the laying on of hands as one of the six foundational principles of the Christian life.

Why does God choose to work through the laying on of human hands? Why does He not just release His anointing directly to each believer? I believe God imparts His power from one believer to another in this way to demonstrate the need for unity in the body of Christ. God does not want us to be "lone ranger" Christians. He wants us to recognize that we need each other. As you pray for God's power, be willing to receive it in any way He desires to impart it.

If you are seeking to receive the Spirit's power, what should you do? The first step is to ask the Lord. Tell him you desire His power. Ask Him to baptize you in the power of the Holy Spirit.

The next step is to seek out a trusted Christian friend or pastor who is filled with the Spirit and have them pray over you to impart the Spirit's power.

If you have done both of these and nothing has yet happened, keep seeking. The things we really want from God we are willing to ask for over and over. Perseverance is a sign of faith.

As you continue to pray, spend time in the Word to increase your understanding of the Spirit and His work. As you do this, hindrances will be removed and you will find yourself more able to freely receive the Spirit's power.

Endnotes

1   Garnet E. Pike, *Receiving the Promise of the Father: How to be Baptized in the Holy Spirit*, (Franklin Springs: LifeSprings Resources, 1997), p. 19-21.

Appendix II

The Gifts of the Spirit

NOTE: This appendix contains material from my book, Experiencing the Spirit, which is available at Glory of Zion.org, and Amazon.com. Experiencing the Spirit is recommended for anyone seeking to walk in the power of the Holy Spirit.

In this appendix, I'd like to share in more detail what spiritual gifts are, and how they are designed to function.

I Corinthians 12 lists what I call the 9 ministry gifts. (I don't think this is a complete list, but it's a good place to begin.) The Greek word Paul uses for these gifts is *charisma,* which means "a gracious gift of God.) These gifts are manifestations of God's power, released to His people to equip them for service. I Cor. 12-14 describes how these gifts function when God's people are gathered in a synaxis.

In I Cor. 12:8-10 we see the Holy Spirit distributing these gifts to His people when they gather:

> *"To one there is given through the Spirit the word of wisdom, to another the word of knowledge by means of the same Spirit, to another faith by the same Spirit, to another gifts of healing by that one Spirit, to another miraculous powers, to another prophecy, to another distinguishing between spirits, to another speaking in*

> *different kinds of tongues, and to still another the interpretation of tongues."*

I like to think of these ministry gifts as channels through which the power of God flows. When you are empowered by the Spirit, that power begins to flow through you in the various *charisma* of the Spirit. Let's see what they are.

1. The Word of Wisdom. – Wisdom means "skill in living." It's the ability to solve problems and deal skillfully with situations to bring about the desired outcome. The Word of Wisdom is revelation from God that provides supernatural wisdom. Kevin Conner calls it "a flash revelation given by the Spirit."[1]

Owen Weston describes it as an "instant insight" that shows "how a given situation or need is to be resolved or helped or healed." [2]

A good Biblical example of this gift is found in Mark 12:14-17. The Pharisees thought they had devised the perfect trap for Jesus. They asked Him if it was right for God's people to pay taxes to Caesar. They knew if He said "yes," He would alienate the Jewish people, who hated the Romans. If He said "no" the Romans would arrest Him for teaching the people not to pay their taxes.

In this seemingly "no win" situation, however, Jesus found a unique answer. Operating in supernatural wisdom from the Holy Spirit, Jesus demanded that the Pharisees tell Him whose image was on a Roman coin. When they said, "Caesar's" His instruction was, "Give to Caesar what belongs to Caesar and give to God what belongs to God."

The Pharisees fully understood what Jesus was saying. Even as that coin bore Caesar's image, every human being carries God's image. We can give to Caesar the taxes he demands, but God demands our heart. The wisdom of Jesus' answer was so profound it left His adversaries without a response. Mark tells us "they were amazed at Him." That's the Word of Wisdom in operation.

2. The Word of Knowledge – The Word of Knowledge is not the ability to study, research or gain knowledge through natural means. It is a Word from God that brings knowledge. Owen Weston calls it "a revelation of facts about a person or situation which is not learned through the efforts of the natural mind, but is a fragment of knowledge freely given by God. . ."[3]

An example of this gift in Jesus' ministry is found in John 4:16-17. In conversing with the woman at the well, Jesus received from the Spirit a piece of information He had no natural way of knowing: She has had five husbands and was not married to the man she was presently living with. That piece of information broke through her pretense and opened the door for revival in an entire village.

3. Faith – Peter Wagner describes the gift of faith as the ability, "to discern with extraordinary confidence the will and purposes of God for the future of His work."[4]

When you operate in the gift of faith, you KNOW what God desires, and are supremely CONFIDENT that, no matter how negative the circumstances seem to be, God will make it possible.

In 1992 God told my wife and I to take our three children with us on a mission trip to Ukraine. After much prayer, we felt we had clearly heard the Lord, so we began making preparations for the trip, applying for their passports, etc. . . . but were met by delays at every point.

The first problem was financial. The total cost of the trip was over $10,000. We sent out letters to the people who usually support our ministry, and money slowly began to come in, but nothing near what we needed. One week before we were due to leave we were still $5,000 short. We knew if we went forward with the trip we could end up $5,000 in debt.

The other problem was with our visas. We could not apply for the visas until all of the children had passports and the passport for one of our children was several weeks late in arriving. When that passport finally came, we sent off the application for the visas, but again were met with a long delay.

One week before we were due to leave, we still had no visas. For travel into the C.I.S. (the former Soviet Union) at that time, you could not board the plane without proper visas in hand. If the day of the flight came and we had no visas, we would simply have forfeited the $10,000 we spent on plane tickets.

The deadline to cancel the trip and get a refund on the tickets came five days before we were due to leave. As that day approached, our friends cautioned us that we could end up deeply in debt and still be unable to make the trip if the visas did not arrive.

We went before the Lord in prayer and the Lord spoke a clear word to us, "You WILL go." It was a clear and unambiguous word. I remember exactly where I was when He spoke it. And through that word, God released to us the gift of faith. No matter how impossible the situation looked, we knew God had said we would *go*, and were certain that somehow God would make it possible.

We committed to go, and within two days the remaining $5,000 came in. That was a real encouragement, but we still had no visas.

Every day we called the visa office in Dallas, but every day we received the same reply. The visas had not yet arrived, but could come any day. The night before we were scheduled to leave we packed all the suitcases and set them in the hallway just inside our front door. We still had no visas.

We were scheduled to leave for the airport at 9:00 the next morning, but knew we could not get on the plane without visas. At 8:30 A.M. the morning of the flight, the phone rang. It was the visa office. The visas had come in. They told us they would send a courier to the airport to meet us at the ticket counter with our visas.

That trip was a tremendous time of ministry and had a life-changing impact on our children, but more than that, it was a tremendous testimony to God's faithfulness to His promise. Looking back, I am amazed we had the faith to walk through that situation. The faith we exercised did not come from our natural ability. It was God's gracious supernatural provision, the gift of faith.

4. Healings – Leslie Flynn defines the gift of healing as "The ability to intervene in a supernatural way as an instrument for the curing of illness and restoration of health."[5]

It should be noted that in the Greek text, both the word "gift" and the word "healing" are in the plural. It literally says there are gifts of healings. That means God gives a variety of healing gifts. I've found that some people are gifted to heal specific kinds of infirmity. Peter Wagner had a particular gift to pray for people with bad backs. Because there are a variety of healing gifts, I've found that healing is often most effectively done in a team, where people with various kinds of healing gifts pray together. Healing can also include the ability to drive out demons. Much of Jesus' ministry involved various kinds of healing.

5. Miracles (*Dunamis*, or Power) – The word translated "miracles" here is the Greek word, *dunamis*, which is usually translated "power." It is a reference to the supernatural power of God. Frank Damazio defines this gift as the ability to perform "what is naturally impossible through the power of God."[6]

R.M. Riggs describes it as "an orderly intervention in the regular operations of nature."[7]

Technically speaking, a miracle is not the suspension of natural law, but the overcoming of the forces of nature through the application of divine power.

The ministry of Jesus provides many illustrations of this gift: walking on water, multiplying resources, raising the dead, etc.

6. Prophecy – Peter Wagner defines prophecy as the ability "to receive and communicate an immediate message of God to His people through a divinely-anointed utterance."[8]

Prophecy is not the same as preaching. Prophecy brings new revelation from God, expressing God's mind and heart about a current situation.

7. Distinguishing Spirits – The gift of distinguishing or discerning spirits is not the same as "discernment." Discerning spirits involves the supernatural ability to discern the forces in the spiritual realm that are influencing activities in the natural realm. Frank Damazio defines it as the ability to recognize "what spirit (divine, evil or human) is causing a certain manifestation or activity."[9]

When Jesus turned to Peter in Matthew 16:23 and said, "Get behind me, Satan." He was looking beyond the natural realm into the spiritual. He recognized that Peter was, at that moment, being influenced in his thoughts and words by Satan. Discerning the demonic spirit behind Peter's statement, Jesus addressed Satan directly and rebuked him.

A person operating in the discerning of spirits can often tell, by looking, what demonic forces are afflicting or influencing an individual.

8. Tongues – The gift of tongues is the ability to "speak by the Spirit in a language that he has not previously learned."[10]

The person speaking in tongues is usually not aware of the meaning of the tongues message.

9. Interpretation of Tongues – The gift of interpretation of tongues is "The divine enablement to make known to the body the message of one who is speaking in tongues."[11]

The interpretation of a tongue is not necessarily a word-for-word translation, but rather a prophetic interpretation of what the tongue is communicating. One who interprets tongues may hear the actual words in English as the tongue is being spoken. At other times, they simply get the "sense" of what is being said.

Levels of Operation

I Cor. 12 indicates these nine ministry gifts operate on two levels.

The first level on which these gifts operate is that of a momentary unction or anointing. At a given point in time, the Spirit of God may release an anointing through one of His people to operate in any of these gifts.

We see this level of operation described in I Cor. 12:7-11. In this passage, Paul describes the situation of a group of Christians coming together in a synaxis. He says that as God's people come together (assuming there is freedom for the gifts to operate) God may give to one person gifts of healing, to another He may give an anointing to prophecy, to another He may give a tongue, etc. God sovereignly manifests His gifts. His people can never know which gifts will be manifested through which person.

On this level, all of these gifts are available to all Christians. On a given occasion, the Spirit can manifest *any* gift through *any* Christian who is open to it. I Cor. 14 makes it clear that in this context ALL can speak in tongues (14:18, 26), ALL can interpret (14:18), ALL can prophecy (14:26,31), etc. I Cor. 14:26 indicates we should all come to church prepared to function in any of the gifts.

Because of this, it is quite possible for a Christian to become proficient in many of the gifts. We know from the book of Acts and I Cor. 14 that Paul's primary ministry was as an apostle, yet he frequently healed the sick, cast out demons, prophesied, spoke in tongues, taught, received words of knowledge, etc. (See, for example, I Cor. 14:6,18).

On several occasions, all Christians are strongly exhorted to seek to operate in all of the gifts and to pray for additional gifts (I Cor 12:31, 14:1, 14:13, 14:39).

The second level on which the charisma operate is that of an ongoing ministry. (See I Cor. 12:27-31.) While any Spirit-filled Christian MAY operate in any of these gifts on occasion, God will give each obedient Christian an ongoing ministry in at least one of these areas.

Appendix II

When God calls a believer to function in one of these gifts on a regular basis, that gift becomes, "their gift" or "their ministry." Some will have an ongoing ministry of healing, others of teaching, others of prophesying, etc. On this level, I Cor. 12:27-31 indicates no one ministry will be given to all Christians. (Not all will be prophets or teachers or healers, etc.)

Endnotes

1   Kevin J. Conner, *The Church in the New Testament*, (Portland: Bible Temple Publishing, 1989), p. 214

2   Owen Weston, *Your Job Description From God: Spiritual Gifts, A Guide for the Development of Lay Ministries*, (Franklin Springs: LifeSprings Resources, 1996), p. 95.

3   Ibid., p. 97

4   C. Peter Wagner, *Your Spiritual Gifts Can Help Your Church Grow, Fifteenth Anniversary Edition Fully Revised and Updated*, (Ventura: Regal Books, a Division of Gospel Light, 1994), p. 146.

5   Leslie B. Flynn, *Nineteen Gifts of the Spirit: Which Do You Have? Are You Using Them?* (Wheaton: Victor Books, 1974), p. 170.

6   Frank Damazio, *The Making of a Leader*, (Portland: Trilogy Productions, 1988), p. 49.

7   R. M. Riggs, *The Spirit Himself*, (Springfield: Gospel Publishing House, 1949), p. 148, quoted in Owen Weston, *Your Job Description From God: Spiritual Gifts, A Guide for the Development of Lay Ministries*, (LifeSprings Resources, 1996), p. 102.

8   Wagner, *Your Spiritual Gifts Can Help Your Church Grow*, p. 200.

9   Damazio, *The Making of a Leader*, p. 50.

10   Ibid.

11   Bruce Bugbee, *Networking (Leaders Guide)*, (Pasadena: Charles E. Fuller Institute of Evangelism and Church Growth. 1989), p. 53, quoted in Owen Weston, *Your Job Description From God: Spiritual Gifts, A Guide for the Development of Lay Ministries*, (LifeSprings Resources, 1996), p. 112.

Appendix III

Establishing a Synaxis

If you lead a home group or house church, it's very easy to transition that group into a New Testament synaxis where spiritual gifts can be nurtured. Here are some suggestions:

1. Begin by teaching about the gifts, and the way gifts operate in the church. (You might want to lead them in a study of this book!)

2. Set aside time for the purpose of learning to exercise the gifts. If your usual format is a Bible study, you may wish to have a refreshment break after the study, then regather for the synaxis.

3. The group should have clear leadership. While there must be freedom, it's not a "free-for-all."

4. The leader should establish an open, accepting atmosphere for the meeting. People need to know it's OK to make mistakes. They need to know if they think they hear God, it is OK to try to share it. At the same time, the leader needs to have the authority and firmness to keep things on track. If someone is disorderly, monopolizing the meeting, or doing something that may be harm-

ful to others, they must be corrected.

5. I Cor. 14:26 stresses that each person is to come prepared. This means spending time with the Lord at some point before the meeting to try to hear what God is saying. Members of the group should come prepared to share, not just to receive.

6. It's also good to establish a sense of covenant community by sharing the Lord's supper. This may also include sharing a meal, even if it's just a light snack.

7. At the beginning of the meeting, have a time of praise and worship. During this time, be sensitive and seek the Spirit's presence. Maintain an atmosphere of worship. When the leader senses the presence of the Spirit, he (or she) should pray and invite the Spirit of God to manifest Himself through His gifts.

8. Following the instructions of I Cor. 14, give people the freedom to share. It may be a passage of Scripture, a song, a prophetic word, or a testimony. If a prophetic word is given, encourage the group to give feedback by saying, "amen" if they sense the word is right. This gives the speaker instant feedback so they can know if they are ministering effectively. Don't be afraid of periods of silence. Learn to wait on the Lord and gain sensitivity to His presence. Try to sense the "flow" of the Spirit, and discern the overall message the Spirit desires to communicate at that meeting.

9. Point out to the people what the Spirit is doing. Help them recognize when

Appendix III

the Spirit has "come upon" someone in the group. Have them pray for those the Spirit is ministering to.

10. At some point, ask if there is anyone sick or in need. As the Spirit leads, have the group gather around and lay hands on the sick person and pray for healing.

The first time you have such a meeting, people may be a little uncomfortable. That's OK. Any time you try something new, some people will be uneasy. Meet together in a group like this weekly for several months and you will be surprised how quickly you will grow in your ability to function in the gifts of the Spirit.